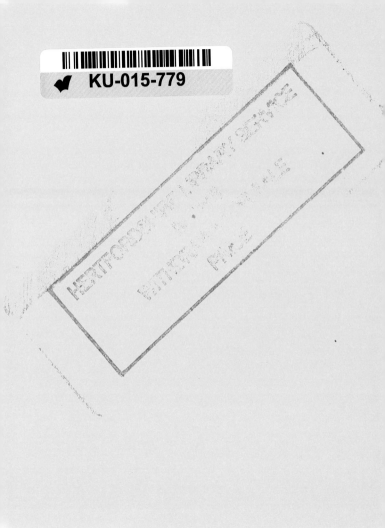

chocolate

100 everyday recipes

First published in 2011
LOVE FOOD is an imprint of Parragon Books Ltd

Parragon
Queen Street House
4 Queen Street
Bath BA1 1HE, UK

Copyright © Parragon Books Ltd 2011

LOVE FOOD and the accompanying heart device is a registered trade mark of Parragon Books Ltd in Australia, the UK, USA, India and the EU

ISBN: 978-1-4454-4284-6

Printed in China

Produced by Ivy Contract
Cover photography by Mike Cooper
Cover image home economy and food styling by Lincoln Jefferson

Notes for the Reader

This book uses both metric and imperial measurements. Follow the same units of measurement throughout; do not mix metric and imperial. All spoon measurements are level: teaspoons are assumed to be 5 ml, and tablespoons are assumed to be 15 ml. Unless otherwise stated, milk is assumed to be full fat, eggs and individual vegetables are medium, and pepper is freshly ground black pepper.

The times given are an approximate guide only. Preparation times differ according to the techniques used by different people and the cooking times may also vary from those given. Optional ingredients, variations or serving suggestions have not been included in the calculations.

Recipes using raw or very lightly cooked eggs should be avoided by infants, the elderly, pregnant women, convalescents and anyone suffering from an illness. Pregnant and breastfeeding women are advised to avoid eating peanuts and peanut products. Sufferers from nut allergies should be aware that some of the ready-made ingredients used in the recipes in this book may contain nuts. Always check the packaging before use.

Vegetarians should be aware that some of the prepared ingredients used in the recipes in this book may contain animal products.

Picture acknowledgments
The publisher would like to thank the following for permission to reproduce copyright material
Front cover: Chocolate pudding © Dennis Gottlieb/Getty Images

chocolate

introduction

The very word 'chocolate' almost has a magic about it and those who love it will agree unanimously that the taste is quite definitely magical.

The remarkable story of chocolate dates back to the 7th century, when the cocoa tree, Theobroma cacao, was cultivated by the Maya of Central America. This ancient civilization established a flourishing trade, even using the cocoa bean as currency. The explorer Christopher Columbus took the cocoa bean to Spain in 1502, and Hernán Cortés, who conquered Mexico for Spain, soon afterwards got an idea of what to do with this curious object when the Aztec Emperor Montezuma introduced him to xocotlatl, a drink made of crushed, roasted cocoa beans and cold water. This bitter-tasting brew soon evolved into something more pleasant when it was served hot with a flavouring of vanilla, spices, honey and sugar.

By the late 17th century, Europe and beyond had fallen under the spell of the 'hot chocolate' drink, but it is a 19th-century Dutch chemist, Coenraad Van Houten, whom we have to thank for chocolate that we can eat. This veritable hero invented a method of producing pure cocoa butter and a hard 'cake' that could be milled to produce cocoa 'powder' for flavouring. Within a very short time, the chocolate industry was founded, going from strength to strength as different countries began to produce smooth, melt-in-the-mouth chocolate bars.

Today – to our delight – there is no end to the creative ways in which chocolate is used in cooking. Puddings, cakes, biscuits, chilled desserts, ice creams – they all seem to have a little extra appeal when they include chocolate.

If you are one of the world's many chocoholics, you'll love this book. Just dip in and be indulgent!

puddings

toffee chocolate puff tarts

ingredients

serves 12

375 g/13 oz ready-rolled
    puff pastry
140 g/5 oz plain chocolate,
    broken into pieces
300 ml/10 fl oz double cream
50 g/1¾ oz caster sugar
4 egg yolks
60 ml/2 fl oz ready-made
    toffee sauce
cocoa powder, for dusting
whipped cream, to serve

method

1 Line the bases of a 12-hole non-stick muffin tin with
discs of parchment paper.

2 Cut out twelve 5-cm/2-inch circles from the edge of
the pastry and cut the remainder into 12 strips. Roll the
strips to half their thickness and line the sides of each
hole with 1 strip. Put a disc of pastry in each base, and
press well together to seal and make a tart case. Prick
the bases and chill in the refrigerator for 30 minutes.

3 While the pastry is chilling, melt the chocolate in
a heatproof bowl set over a saucepan of gently
simmering water. Remove the bowl from the heat, cool
slightly, then stir in the cream. Beat the sugar and egg
yolks together and mix well with the melted chocolate.

4 Remove the muffin tin from the refrigerator and put
a teaspoonful of the toffee sauce into each tart case.
Divide the chocolate mixture between the tarts and
bake in a preheated oven, 200°C/400°F/Gas Mark 6,
for 20–25 minutes, turning the tray around halfway
through cooking, until just set.

5 Remove from the oven and cool the tarts in the tin.
Carefully remove the tarts from the tin, leaving behind
the parchment paper. Dust the tarts with cocoa
powder and serve with whipped cream.

profiteroles

ingredients

serves 4

choux pastry

70 g/2½ oz unsalted butter,
    plus extra for greasing
200 ml/7 fl oz water
100 g/3½ oz plain flour
3 eggs, beaten

cream filling

300 ml/10 fl oz double cream
3 tbsp caster sugar
1 tsp vanilla extract

chocolate & brandy sauce

125 g/4½ oz plain chocolate,
    broken into small pieces
35 g/1¼ oz unsalted butter
90 ml/3 fl oz water
2 tbsp brandy

method

1 Lightly grease a large baking tray. To make the pastry, place the butter and water in a saucepan and bring to the boil. Meanwhile, sift the flour into a bowl. Turn off the heat and beat in the flour until smooth. Cool for 5 minutes. Beat in enough of the eggs to give the mixture a soft, dropping consistency.

2 Transfer to a piping bag fitted with a 1-cm/½-inch plain nozzle. Pipe small balls onto the prepared baking tray. Bake in a preheated oven, 200°C/400°F/Gas Mark 6, for 25 minutes.

3 Remove from the oven. Pierce each ball with a skewer to let the steam escape.

4 To make the filling, whip the cream, sugar and vanilla extract together. Cut the pastry balls across the middle, then fill with cream.

5 To make the sauce, gently melt the chocolate, butter and water together in a small saucepan, stirring constantly, until smooth. Stir in the brandy.

6 Pile the profiteroles into individual serving dishes, pour over the sauce and serve.

chocolate cherry clafoutis

ingredients

serves 6–8

butter, for greasing
450 g/1 lb black cherries, stoned
25 g/1 oz golden granulated sugar
3 eggs
55 g/2 oz golden caster sugar
55 g/2 oz self-raising flour
2 tbsp cocoa powder
150 ml/5 fl oz double cream
300 ml/10 fl oz milk
2 tbsp kirsch (optional)
lightly whipped cream,
    to serve

method

1 Lightly grease a 23-cm/9-inch square ovenproof dish. Arrange the cherries in the prepared dish, sprinkle with the granulated sugar and set aside.

2 Put the eggs and caster sugar in a bowl and whisk together until light and frothy. Sift the flour and cocoa powder into a separate bowl and add, all at once, to the egg mixture. Beat in thoroughly, then whisk in the cream followed by the milk and kirsch, if using. Pour the mixture over the cherries.

3 Bake in a preheated oven, 190°C/375°F/Gas Mark 5, for 50–60 minutes, until slightly risen and set in the centre

4 Serve warm with cream.

chocolate nut strudel

ingredients

serves 6

200 g/7 oz mixed chopped nuts
115 g/4 oz plain chocolate,
    chopped
115 g/4 oz milk chocolate,
    chopped
115 g/4 oz white chocolate,
    chopped
200 g/7 oz filo pastry,
    thawed if frozen
150 g/5½ oz butter, melted,
    plus extra for greasing
3 tbsp golden syrup

method

1 Lightly grease a baking tray.

2 Reserve 1 tablespoon of the nuts. Place the remaining nuts in a bowl and mix together with the three types of chocolate.

3 Place a sheet of filo pastry on a clean tea towel. Brush the sheet of filo with the melted butter, drizzle with a little golden syrup and sprinkle with a little of the nut and chocolate mixture. Repeat the layers until you have used up all the filo pastry, butter, nuts and chocolate and most of the golden syrup.

4 Use the tea towel to help you carefully roll up the strudel and place on the prepared baking tray. Drizzle with a little more golden syrup and sprinkle with the reserved nuts. Bake in a preheated oven, 190°C/375°F/Gas Mark 5, for 20–25 minutes. If the nuts start to brown too much, cover the strudel with a sheet of foil. Serve warm.

chocolate queen of puddings

ingredients

serves 4

50 g/1¾ oz plain chocolate
450 ml/16 fl oz chocolate-
    flavoured milk
100 g/3½ oz fresh white or
    wholemeal breadcrumbs
125 g/4½ oz caster sugar
2 eggs, separated
100 g/4 oz black cherry jam

method

1 Break the chocolate into small pieces and place in
  a saucepan with the chocolate-flavoured milk. Heat
  gently, stirring until the chocolate melts. Bring almost
  to the boil, then remove the saucepan from the heat.

2 Place the breadcrumbs in a large mixing bowl with
  25 g/1 oz of the sugar. Pour over the chocolate milk
  and mix well. Beat in the egg yolks.

3 Spoon into a 1.2-litre/2-pint ovenproof dish and
  bake in a preheated oven, 180°C/350°F/Gas Mark 4,
  for 25–30 minutes, or until set and firm to the touch.

4 Whisk the egg whites in a large grease-free bowl until
  soft peaks form. Gradually whisk in the remaining
  caster sugar and whisk until you have a glossy,
  thick meringue.

5 Spread the black cherry jam over the surface of the
  chocolate mixture and pile the meringue on top.
  Return the dish to the oven for about 15 minutes
  or until the meringue is crisp and golden. Serve.

chocolate apple lattice tart

ingredients

serves 6

pastry

200 g/7 oz plain flour,
    plus extra for dusting
2 tbsp cocoa powder
3 tbsp caster sugar
100 g/3½ oz unsalted butter,
    diced, plus extra for greasing
1–2 egg yolks, beaten

filling

225 ml/8 fl oz double cream
2 eggs, beaten
1 tsp ground cinnamon
115 g/4 oz plain chocolate, grated
4 eating apples, peeled, sliced and
    brushed with lemon juice
3 tbsp demerara sugar

method

1 To make the pastry, sift the flour and cocoa into a food processor. Stir in the sugar, then add the butter and process until the mixture resembles fine breadcrumbs. Stir in enough egg yolk to form a dough. Form into a ball, wrap in foil and chill for 45 minutes.

2 Grease a 20-cm/8-inch loose-based round tart tin. Roll out the dough on a lightly floured work surface and use three quarters of it to line the prepared tin.

3 For the filling, beat together the cream, the eggs (reserving a little for glazing), cinnamon and chocolate. Place the apples in a bowl, pour over the cream mixture and stir. Spoon the mixture into the prepared tart tin, then sprinkle over the demerara sugar.

4 Roll out the remaining dough and cut into long strips, then arrange over the tart to form a lattice pattern. Brush the pastry strips with the reserved egg yolk, then bake in a preheated oven, 180°C/350°F/Gas Mark 4, for 40–45 minutes.

5 Remove the tart from the oven and leave to cool to room temperature. Serve.

fine chocolate tart

ingredients

serves 6

pastry

150 g/5 oz plain flour
2 tsp cocoa powder
2 tsp icing sugar
pinch of salt
50 g/1¾ oz cold butter, cut into
    pieces, plus extra for greasing
1 egg yolk
ice-cold water

ganache filling

200 g/7 oz plain chocolate with
    70% cocoa solids
25 g/1 oz unsalted butter, softened
250 ml/9 fl oz double cream
1 tsp dark rum (optional)
white and dark chocolate curls,
    to serve

method

1 Lightly grease a 23-cm/9-inch loose-based fluted tart tin. To make the pastry, sift the flour, cocoa, icing sugar and salt into a food processor, add the butter and process until the mixture resembles fine breadcrumbs. Tip the mixture into a large bowl, add the egg yolk and just enough ice-cold water to bring the pastry together. Turn out onto a work surface dusted with more flour and cocoa and roll out the pastry about 7.5 cm/3 inches larger than the tin. Carefully lift the pastry into the tin and press to fit. Roll the rolling pin over the prepared tin to neaten the edges and trim the excess pastry. Fit a piece of baking parchment into the tart shell, fill with baking beans, and chill in the refrigerator for 30 minutes.

2 Remove the pastry case from the refrigerator and bake in a preheated oven, 190°C/375°F/Gas Mark 5, for 15 minutes, then remove the beans and paper and bake for a further 5–10 minutes. Set aside to cool.

3 To make the ganache filling, chop the chocolate and put in a bowl with the softened butter. Bring the cream to the boil, then pour onto the chocolate, stirring well, add the rum (if using) and stir again to make sure the chocolate is melted. Pour into the pastry case and chill in the refrigerator for 3 hours. Serve decorated with chocolate curls.

white chocolate & cardamom tart

ingredients

serves 6

pastry
150 g/5 oz plain flour
pinch of salt
75 g/2½ oz cold butter,
    cut into pieces, plus extra
    for greasing
ice-cold water

filling
seeds of 8 cardamom pods,
    crushed to a powder
350 g/12 oz white chocolate,
    chopped into small pieces
2 pieces fine leaf gelatine
cold water
425 ml/15 fl oz whipping cream
white chocolate curls, to decorate

method

1 Lightly grease a 23-cm/9-inch loose-based fluted tart
tin. To make the pastry, sift the flour and salt into a food
processor, add the butter and process until the mixture
resembles fine breadcrumbs. Tip into a large bowl
and add just enough ice-cold water to bring the pastry
together. Turn out the pastry onto a lightly floured work
surface and roll out to 7.5 cm/3 inches larger than the
tin. Carefully lift the pastry into the tin and press to fit.
Roll the rolling pin over the prepared tin and press
to fit. Trim the excess pastry. Fit a piece of baking
parchment into the tart shell, fill with baking beans,
and chill in the refrigerator for 30 minutes.

2 Remove the pastry case from the refrigerator and bake
blind in a preheated oven, 190°C/375°F/Gas Mark 5,
for 15 minutes. Remove the beans and paper and bake
for a further 5–10 minutes. Set aside to cool.

3 Put the crushed cardamom in a large bowl with the
chocolate. Soak the gelatine in a little cold water in a
bowl for 5 minutes, then stir over a pan of simmering
water until dissolved. Heat the cream until just boiling,
then pour over the chocolate, whisking until the
chocolate has melted and add the gelatine. Cool, then
pour into the tart shell and chill in the refrigerator for
at least 3 hours. Serve decorated with chocolate curls.

chocolate fudge tart

ingredients

serves 6–8

350 g/12 oz ready-made
    shortcrust pastry
flour, for sprinkling
icing sugar, for dusting

filling

140 g/5 oz plain chocolate,
    finely chopped
175 g/6 oz butter, diced
350 g/12 oz golden granulated
    sugar
100 g/3½ oz plain flour
½ tsp vanilla extract
6 eggs, beaten

to decorate

150 ml/5 fl oz whipped cream
ground cinnamon

method

1 Roll out the pastry on a lightly floured work surface and
use to line a 20-cm/8-inch deep loose-based tart tin.
Prick the base lightly with a fork, then line with foil
and fill with baking beans. Bake in a preheated oven,
200°C/400°F/Gas Mark 6, for 12–15 minutes, or until
the pastry no longer looks raw. Remove the beans and
foil and bake for a further 10 minutes, or until the pastry
is firm to the touch. Allow to cool. Reduce the oven
temperature to 180°C/350°F/Gas Mark 4.

2 To make the filling, place the chocolate and butter in
a heatproof bowl and set over a saucepan of gently
simmering water until melted. Stir until smooth, then
remove from the heat and set aside to cool. Place the
sugar, flour, vanilla extract and eggs in a separate bowl
and whisk until well blended. Stir in the butter and
chocolate mixture.

3 Pour the filling into the pastry case and bake in the
oven for 50 minutes, or until the filling is just set.
Transfer to a wire rack to cool completely. Dust with
icing sugar before serving with whipped cream
sprinkled lightly with cinnamon.

chocolate chiffon pie

ingredients

serves 8

nut base
225 g/8 oz shelled Brazil nuts
55 g/2 oz granulated sugar
4 tsp melted butter

filling
225 ml/8 fl oz milk
2 tsp powdered gelatine
115 g/4 oz caster sugar
2 eggs, separated
225 g/8 oz plain chocolate,
    roughly chopped
1 tsp vanilla extract
150 ml/5 fl oz double cream
2 tbsp chopped Brazil nuts,
    to decorate

method

1 Process the whole Brazil nuts in a food processor until finely ground. Add the granulated sugar and melted butter and process briefly to combine. Tip the mixture into a 23-cm/9-inch round tart tin and press it onto the base and sides with a spoon. Bake in a preheated oven, 200°C/400°F/Gas Mark 6, for 8–10 minutes, or until light golden brown. Set aside to cool.

2 Pour the milk into a heatproof bowl and sprinkle over the gelatine. Leave it to soften for 2 minutes, then set over a saucepan of gently simmering water. Stir in half of the caster sugar, both the egg yolks and all the chocolate. Stir constantly over low heat for 4–5 minute until the gelatine has dissolved and the chocolate has melted. Remove from the heat and beat until smooth. Stir in the vanilla extract, cover and chill in the refrigerator for 45–60 minutes until starting to set.

3 Whip the cream until stiff, then fold all but 3 tablespoons into the chocolate mixture. Whisk the egg whites in a clean, greasefree bowl until soft peaks form. Add 2 teaspoons of the remaining sugar and whisk until stiff peaks form. Fold in the remaining sugar, then fold the egg whites into the chocolate mixture. Pour the filling into the pastry case and chill in the refrigerator for 3 hours. Decorate the pie with the remaining whipped cream and the chopped nuts before serving.

pecan & chocolate pie

ingredients

serves 6–8

pastry
175 g/6 oz plain flour, plus extra
    for dusting
100 g/3½ oz butter, diced
1 tbsp golden caster sugar
1 egg yolk, beaten with
    1 tbsp water

filling
55 g/2 oz butter
3 tbsp cocoa powder
225 ml/8 fl oz golden syrup
3 eggs
70 g/2½ oz soft dark brown sugar
175 g/6 oz shelled pecan nuts,
    chopped

to serve
whipped cream
ground cinnamon, for dusting

method

1 To make the pastry, sift the flour into a food processor.
   Add the butter and process until the mixture resembles
   fine breadcrumbs, then stir in the caster sugar. Stir in
   the beaten egg yolk. Knead lightly to form a firm
   dough, cover with clingfilm and chill in the refrigerator
   for 1½ hours. Roll out the chilled pastry on a lightly
   floured work surface and use it to line a 20-cm/8-inch
   tart tin.

2 To make the filling, place the butter in a small,
   heavy-based saucepan and heat gently until melted.
   Sift in the cocoa and stir in the syrup. Place the eggs
   and sugar in a large bowl and beat together. Add the
   syrup mixture and the chopped pecan nuts and stir.
   Pour the mixture into the prepared pastry case.

3 Place the pie on a preheated baking sheet and bake in
   a preheated oven, 190°C/375°F/Gas Mark 5, for 35–40
   minutes, or until the filling is just set. Leave it to cool
   slightly and serve warm with a spoonful of whipped
   cream, dusted with ground cinnamon.

mississippi mud pie

ingredients

serves 8

pastry

225 g/8 oz plain flour, plus extra
    for dusting
2 tbsp cocoa powder
150 g/5½ oz butter, cut into pieces
2 tbsp caster sugar
1–2 tbsp cold water

filling

175 g/6 oz cold butter, cut into
    pieces
350 g/12 oz dark brown sugar
4 eggs, lightly beaten
25 g/1 oz cocoa powder, sifted
150 g/5½ oz plain chocolate
300 ml/10 fl oz single cream
1 tsp chocolate extract

to decorate

425 ml/15 fl oz double cream,
    whipped
chocolate flakes and curls

method

1 To make the pastry, sift the flour and cocoa into a food
   processor. Add the butter and process until the mixture
   resembles fine breadcrumbs. Stir in the sugar and
   enough cold water to mix to a soft dough. Wrap the
   dough and chill in the refrigerator for 15 minutes.

2 Roll out the pastry on a lightly floured work surface
   and use to line a 23-cm/9-inch loose-based tart tin
   or ceramic pie dish. Line with baking parchment and
   fill with baking beans. Bake in a preheated oven,
   190°C/375°F/Gas Mark 5, for 15 minutes. Remove
   from the oven and take out the beans and parchment.
   Bake the pastry case for a further 10 minutes.

3 To make the filling, beat the butter and sugar together
   in a bowl and gradually beat in the eggs with the
   cocoa. Melt the chocolate and beat it into the mixture
   with the single cream and the chocolate extract.

4 Reduce the oven temperature to 160°C/325°F/Gas
   Mark 3. Pour the mixture into the pastry case and bake
   for 45 minutes, or until the filling has set gently.

5 Allow the mud pie to cool completely, then transfer it
   to a serving plate, if you like. Cover with the whipped
   cream. Decorate the pie with chocolate flakes and curls
   and then chill until ready to serve.

chocolate crumble pie

ingredients

serves 8

pastry
200 g/7 oz plain flour
1 tsp baking powder
115 g/4 oz unsalted butter,
    cut into small pieces
25 g/1 oz caster sugar
1 egg yolk
1–2 tsp cold water

filling
150 ml/5 fl oz double cream
150 ml/5 fl oz milk
225 g/8 oz plain chocolate,
    chopped
2 eggs

crumble topping
100 g/3½ oz brown sugar
85 g/3 oz toasted pecan nuts
115 g/4 oz plain chocolate
85 g/3 oz amaretti biscuits
1 tsp cocoa powder

method

1 To make the pastry, sift the flour and baking powder into a food processor and add the butter. Process and add the sugar, then add the egg yolk and a little water to bring the pastry together. Turn the pastry out and knead briefly. Wrap the pastry and chill in the refrigerator for 30 minutes.

2 Roll out the pastry and use to line a 23-cm/9-inch loose-based tart tin. Prick the pastry case with a fork. Line with baking parchment and fill with baking beans. Bake in a preheated oven, 190°C/375°F/Gas Mark 5 for 15 minutes. Remove from the oven and take out the beans and parchment. Reduce the oven temperature to 180°C/350°F/Gas Mark 4.

3 Bring the cream and milk to the boil in a saucepan, remove from the heat, and add the chocolate. Stir until melted and smooth. Beat the eggs and add to the chocolate mixture, mix thoroughly and pour into the pastry case. Bake for 15 minutes, remove the pie from the oven and leave it to rest for 1 hour.

4 Place all the topping ingredients in the food processor and process to create a chunky crumble topping. Sprinkle over the pie, and serve.

chocolate blueberry pies

ingredients

serves 10

pastry
200 g/7 oz plain flour
55 g/2 oz cocoa powder
55 g/2 oz caster sugar
pinch of salt
125 g/4½ oz butter,
   cut into small pieces
1 egg yolk
1–2 tbsp cold water

sauce
200 g/7 oz blueberries
2 tbsp crème de cassis
1¼ tbsp icing sugar, sifted

filling
140 g/5 oz plain chocolate,
   broken into pieces
225 ml/7½ fl oz double cream
150 ml/5 fl oz soured cream

method

1 To make the pastry, place the flour, cocoa, sugar and salt in a food processor and add the butter. Process until the mixture resembles breadcrumbs. Add the egg yolk and a little water to form a dough. Wrap the dough and chill in the refrigerator for 30 minutes.

2 Remove the pastry from the refrigerator and roll out. Use to line 10 x 10-cm/4-inch tart tins. Freeze for 30 minutes. Bake the pastry cases in a preheated oven, 180°C/350°F/Gas Mark 4, for 15–20 minutes. Set aside to cool.

3 To make the sauce, place the blueberries, cassis and icing sugar in a saucepan and warm through so that the berries become shiny but do not burst. Set aside to cool.

4 To make the filling, melt the chocolate in a heatproof bowl set over a saucepan of simmering water, then cool slightly. Whip the cream until stiff and fold in the soured cream and chocolate.

5 Remove the pastry cases to serving plates and divide the chocolate filling between them. Smooth the chocoate surface with a spatula, then top with the blueberries. Serve with the sauce.

chocolate ginger puddings

ingredients

serves 4

100 g/3½ oz soft margarine,
   plus extra for greasing
100 g/3½ oz self-raising flour,
   sifted
100 g/3½ oz caster sugar
2 eggs
25 g/1 oz cocoa powder, sifted
25 g/1 oz plain chocolate
50 g/1¾ oz stem ginger,
   plus extra to decorate
demerara sugar, for topping

chocolate custard

2 egg yolks
1 tbsp caster sugar, plus
   extra for dusting
1 tbsp cornflour
300 ml/10 fl oz milk
100 g/3½ oz plain chocolate,
   broken into pieces

method

1 Lightly grease 4 small individual ovenproof bowls.

2 Place the margarine, flour, sugar, eggs and cocoa in a bowl and beat together until well combined and smooth. Chop the chocolate and stem ginger and stir into the mixture, ensuring they are well combined.

3 Divide the cake mixture between the prepared bowls and smooth the tops. Cover the bowls with discs of baking parchment and cover with a pleated sheet of foil to seal. Half-fill a steamer with water and bring to the boil. Steam the puddings for 45 minutes until the sponges are cooked and springy to the touch.

4 Meanwhile, make the custard. Beat the egg yolks, sugar and cornflour together to form a smooth paste. Heat the milk until boiling and pour over the egg mixture. Return to the saucepan and cook over very low heat, stirring until thick. Remove from the heat and beat in the chocolate. Stir until the chocolate melts.

5 Lift the chocolate gingers from the steamer, run a knife around the edge of the bowls and carefully turn out onto serving plates. Dust each pudding with sugar and drizzle the chocolate custard over the top. Decorate with stem ginger and serve. Serve the remaining chocolate custard separately.

sticky chocolate puddings

ingredients

serves 6

125 g/4$\frac{1}{2}$ oz butter, softened,
    plus extra for greasing
150 g/5$\frac{1}{2}$ oz brown sugar
3 eggs, beaten
pinch of salt
25 g/1 oz cocoa powder
125 g/4$\frac{1}{2}$ oz self-raising flour
25 g/1 oz plain chocolate,
    finely chopped
75 g/2$\frac{3}{4}$ oz white chocolate,
    finely chopped

sauce

150 ml/5 fl oz double cream
75 g/2$\frac{3}{4}$ oz brown sugar
25 g/1 oz butter

method

1 Lightly grease 6 individual 175-ml/6-fl oz ovenproof pudding moulds.

2 Cream the butter and sugar together in a bowl until pale and fluffy. Beat in the eggs a little at a time, beating well after each addition. Sift the salt, cocoa and flour into the creamed mixture and fold in. Stir in the chopped chocolate until evenly combined throughout.

3 Divide the mixture between the prepared moulds. Lightly grease 6 squares of foil and use them to cover the tops of the moulds, pressing around the edges to seal. Place the moulds in a roasting pan and pour in boiling water to come halfway up the sides of the moulds. Bake in a preheated oven, 180°C/350°F/Gas Mark 4, for 50 minutes, or until a skewer inserted into the centre of the sponges comes out clean. Remove the moulds from the roasting pan and set aside.

4 To make the sauce, put the cream, sugar and butter into a saucepan and bring to the boil over a gentle heat. Simmer the sauce gently until the sugar has completely dissolved.

5 To serve, run a knife around the edge of each sponge, then turn out onto serving plates. Serve immediately with the jug of sauce for pouring over.

individual chocolate puddings

ingredients

serves 4

100 g/3½ oz caster sugar
3 eggs
75 g/2¾ oz plain flour
50 g/1¾ oz cocoa powder
100 g/3½ oz unsalted butter,
   melted, plus extra for greasing
100 g/3½ oz plain chocolate,
   melted

chocolate sauce

25 g/1 oz unsalted butter
100 g/3½ oz plain chocolate,
   broken into pieces
75 ml/2½ fl oz water
1 tbsp caster sugar
1 tbsp coffee-flavoured liqueur,
   such as Kahlúa
coffee beans, to decorate

method

1 Grease 4 small heatproof bowls with butter. To make
   the puddings, put the sugar and eggs into a heatproof
   bowl and place over a saucepan of simmering water.
   Whisk for about 10 minutes until frothy. Remove the
   bowl from the heat and fold in the flour and cocoa.
   Fold in the butter, then the chocolate. Mix well.

2 Spoon the mixture into the prepared bowls and cover
   with waxed paper. Top with foil and secure with string.
   Place in a large saucepan filled with enough simmering
   water to reach halfway up the sides of the bowls.
   Steam for about 40 minutes, or until cooked through.

3 About 2–3 minutes before the end of the cooking
   time, make the sauce. Put the butter, chocolate, water
   and sugar into a small saucepan and warm over a low
   heat, stirring constantly, until melted. Stir in the liqueur.

4 Remove the puddings from the heat, turn out onto
   serving dishes, and pour over the sauce. Decorate with
   coffee beans and serve.

cappuccino soufflé puddings

ingredients

serves 6

butter, for greasing
2 tbsp golden caster sugar,
    plus extra for coating
90 ml/3 fl oz whipping cream
2 tsp instant espresso coffee
    granules
2 tbsp Kahlúa
3 large eggs, separated,
    plus 1 extra egg white
150 g/5½ oz plain chocolate,
    melted and cooled
cocoa powder, for dusting
chocolate-coated biscuits,
    to serve

method

1 Lightly grease the sides of 6 x 175-ml/6-fl oz ramekins with butter and coat with caster sugar. Place the ramekins on a baking sheet.

2 Place the cream in a small, heavy-based saucepan and heat gently. Stir in the coffee until it has dissolved, then stir in the Kahlúa. Divide the coffee mixture between the prepared ramekins.

3 Place the egg whites in a clean, greasefree bowl and whisk until soft peaks form, then gradually whisk in the sugar until stiff but not dry. Stir the egg yolks and melted chocolate together in a separate bowl, then stir in a little of the whisked egg whites. Gradually fold in the remaining egg whites.

4 Divide the mixture between the dishes. Bake in a preheated oven, 190°C/375°F/Gas Mark 5, for 15 minutes, or until just set. Dust with cocoa and serve immediately with chocolate-coated biscuits.

chocolate zabaglione

ingredients

serves 4

4 egg yolks
55 g/2 oz caster sugar
50 g/1¾ oz plain chocolate
125 ml/4 fl oz Marsala wine
amaretti biscuits, to serve

method

1 Place the egg yolks and caster sugar in a large glass bowl and, using an electric whisk, whisk together until the mixture is very pale.

2 Grate the chocolate finely and, using a spatula, fold into the egg mixture. Fold the Marsala wine into the chocolate mixture.

3 Place the bowl over a saucepan of gently simmering water and set the electric whisk on the lowest speed or swap to a balloon whisk. Cook gently, whisking constantly, until the mixture thickens. Do not overcook or the mixture will curdle.

4 Spoon the hot mixture into four warmed glass dishes or coffee cups. Serve as soon as possible, while it is warm, light and fluffy, with amaretti biscuits.

variation

Add 350 g/12 oz fresh strawberries, cut into quarters. Pour the hot zabaglione over the strawberries and serve.

chocolate fondue

ingredients

serves 6

1 pineapple
1 mango
12 physalis
250 g/9 oz fresh strawberries
250 g/9 oz seedless green
    grapes

fondue

250 g/9 oz plain chocolate,
    broken into pieces
150 ml/5 fl oz double cream
2 tbsp brandy

method

1 Using a sharp knife, peel and core the pineapple, then
   cut the flesh into cubes. Peel the mango and cut the
   flesh into cubes. Peel back the papery outer skin of
   the physalis and twist at the top to make a 'handle'.
   Arrange the fruit on six serving plates and chill in
   the refrigerator.

2 To make the fondue, place the chocolate and cream
   in a fondue pot. Heat gently, stirring constantly, until
   the chocolate has melted. Stir in the brandy until
   blended and the chocolate mixture is smooth.

3 Place the fondue pot over the burner to keep warm.
   To serve, allow each guest to dip the fruit into the
   sauce, using fondue forks or bamboo skewers.

chilled & iced desserts

chocolate hazelnut parfaits

ingredients

serves 6

175 g/6 oz blanched hazelnuts
175 g/6 oz plain chocolate,
    broken into small pieces
600 ml/1 pint double cream
250 g/9 oz icing sugar
3 eggs, separated
6 small fresh mint sprigs,
    to decorate
wafer biscuits, to serve

method

1 Spread out the hazelnuts on a baking tray and toast under a preheated grill for about 5 minutes, shaking the sheet from time to time, until golden all over. Set aside to cool.

2 Put the chocolate in a heatproof bowl set over a saucepan of gently simmering water. Stir over a low heat until melted, then remove from the heat and cool. Put the toasted hazelnuts in a food processor and process until finely ground.

3 Whisk the cream until it is stiff, then fold in the ground hazelnuts and set aside. Add 3 tablespoons of the sugar to the egg yolks and beat for 10 minutes until pale and thick.

4 Whisk the egg whites in a separate bowl until soft peaks form. Whisk in the remaining sugar, a little at a time, until the whites are stiff and glossy. Stir the cooled chocolate into the egg yolk mixture, then fold in the cream and finally, fold in the egg whites. Divide the mixture between six freezerproof timbales o moulds, cover, and freeze for at least 8 hours until firm.

5 Transfer the frozen parfaits to the refrigerator about 10 minutes before serving to soften slightly. Turn out onto individual serving plates, decorate with mint sprigs and serve with wafer biscuits.

chocolate & orange slices

ingredients

serves 8

butter, for greasing

450 g/1 lb plain chocolate,
    broken into pieces

3 small, loose-skinned oranges,
    such as tangerines, mandarins
    or satsumas

4 egg yolks

200 ml/7 fl oz crème fraîche

2 tbsp raisins

300 ml/10 fl oz whipped cream,
    to serve

method

1 Lightly grease a 450-g/1-lb loaf tin and line it with clingfilm. Put the chocolate in a heatproof bowl set over a saucepan of gently simmering water. Stir over a low heat until melted. Remove from the heat and leave to cool slightly.

2 Meanwhile, peel the oranges, removing all traces of pith. Cut the zest into very thin strips. Beat the egg yolks into the chocolate, one at a time, then add most of the orange zest (reserving the rest for decoration), and all the crème fraîche and raisins, and beat until thoroughly combined. Spoon the mixture into the prepared tin, cover with clingfilm and chill in the refrigerator for 3–4 hours, until set.

3 To serve, remove the tin from the refrigerator and turn out the chocolate terrine. Remove the clingfilm and cut the mould into slices. Place a slice on individual serving plates and add whipped cream to serve. Decorate with the remaining orange zest.

white & dark chocolate ice cream

ingredients

serves 4

6 egg yolks
100 g/3½ oz caster sugar
350 ml/12 fl oz milk
175 ml/6 fl oz double cream
100 g/3½ oz plain chocolate,
    chopped
75 g/2¾ oz white chocolate,
    grated or finely chopped
fresh mint leaves, to decorate

method

1 Put the egg yolks and sugar into a large, heatproof bowl and beat until fluffy. Heat the milk, cream and dark chocolate in a saucepan over a low heat, stirring, until melted and almost boiling. Remove from the heat and whisk into the egg mixture. Return to the pan and cook, stirring, over a low heat until thick. Do not let it simmer. Transfer to a heatproof bowl and leave to cool. Cover the bowl with clingfilm and chill in the refrigerator for 1½ hours.

2 Remove from the refrigerator and stir in the white chocolate. Transfer to a freezerproof container and freeze for 1 hour. Remove from the freezer, transfer to a bowl and whisk to break up the ice crystals. Return to the container and freeze for 30 minutes. Repeat twice more, freezing for 30 minutes and whisking each time. Alternatively, transfer the mixture to an ice-cream machine and process for 15 minutes.

3 Scoop into serving bowls, decorate with mint leaves and serve.

white chocolate terrine

ingredients

serves 8

25 g/1 oz granulated sugar
75 ml/2½ fl oz water
300 g/10½ oz white chocolate
3 eggs, separated
300 ml/10 fl oz double cream

to serve
fruit coulis
fresh strawberries

method

1 Line a 450-g/1-lb loaf tin with foil or clingfilm, pressing out as many creases as you can.

2 Place the granulated sugar and water in a heavy-based saucepan and heat gently, stirring until the sugar has dissolved. Bring to the boil and boil for 1–2 minutes until syrupy, then remove from the heat.

3 Break the white chocolate into small pieces and stir it into the hot syrup, continuing to stir until the chocolate has melted and combined with the syrup. Let the mixture cool slightly.

4 Beat the egg yolks into the chocolate mixture. Leave to cool completely.

5 Lightly whip the cream until it is just holding its shape, and fold it into the chocolate mixture.

6 Whisk the egg whites in a greasefree bowl until soft peaks form. Fold the whites into the chocolate mixture. Pour into the prepared loaf tin and freeze overnight.

7 To serve, remove the terrine from the freezer about 10–15 minutes before serving. Turn out of the tin and cut into slices. Serve with fruit coulis and strawberries.

chocolate & vanilla creams

ingredients

serves 4

450 ml/16 fl oz double cream
85g/3 oz caster sugar
1 vanilla pod
200 ml/7 fl oz crème fraîche
2 tsp powdered gelatine
45 ml/1½ fl oz water
50 g/1¾ oz plain chocolate,
  broken into pieces
marbled chocolate caraque,
  chopped, to decorate

method

1 Place the cream and sugar in a saucepan and add the vanilla pod. Heat gently, stirring until the sugar has dissolved, then bring to the boil. Reduce the heat and simmer for 2–3 minutes.

2 Remove the saucepan from the heat and take out the vanilla pod. Stir in the crème fraîche.

3 Sprinkle the gelatine over the water in a small heatproof bowl and let it go spongy, then set over a saucepan of hot water and stir until dissolved. Stir into the cream mixture. Pour half of this mixture into another mixing bowl.

4 Put the plain chocolate in a heatproof bowl over a saucepan of simmering water until melted. Stir the melted chocolate into one half of the cream mixture. Pour the chocolate mixture into four individual glasses or glass serving dishes and chill for 15–20 minutes, until just set. While the chocolate mixture is chilling, keep the vanilla mixture at room temperature.

5 Spoon the vanilla mixture on top of the chocolate mixture and chill until the vanilla cream is set. When ready to serve, decorate with the chopped caraque.

brownie bottom cheesecake

ingredients

serves 12

115 g/4 oz unsalted butter,
    plus extra for greasing
115 g/4 oz plain chocolate
200 g/7 oz caster sugar
2 eggs, beaten
50 ml /2 fl oz milk
115 g/4 oz plain flour, plus
    extra for dusting

topping

500 g/1 lb 2 oz soft cheese
125 g/4½ oz caster sugar
3 eggs, beaten
1 tsp vanilla extract
125 ml/4 fl oz natural yogurt
plain chocolate, melted,
    to drizzle

method

1 Lightly grease and flour a 23-cm/9-inch round
   baking tin.

2 Melt the butter and chocolate in a saucepan over a
   low heat, stirring often, until smooth. Remove from the
   heat and beat in the sugar.

3 Add the eggs and milk, beating well. Stir in the flour,
   mixing just until blended. Spoon into the prepared tin,
   spreading evenly.

4 Bake in a preheated oven, 180°C/350°F/Gas Mark 4,
   for 25 minutes. Remove from the oven while preparing
   the topping. Reduce the oven temperature to
   160°C/325°F/Gas Mark 3.

5 For the topping, beat together the cheese, sugar,
   eggs and vanilla essence until well blended. Stir in the
   yogurt, then pour over the brownie base. Bake for a
   further 45–55 minutes or until the centre is almost set.

6 Run a knife around the edge of the cake to loosen from
   the tin. Leave to cool before removing from the tin.
   Chill in the refrigerator for 4 hours or overnight before
   cutting the cheesecake into slices. Serve drizzled with
   melted chocolate.

tiramisù layers

ingredients

serves 6

150 ml/5 fl oz double cream
400 g/14 oz mascarpone cheese
300 g/10 oz plain chocolate,
    broken into pieces
400 ml/14 fl oz hot black coffee
55 g/2 oz caster sugar
90 ml/3 fl oz dark rum or brandy
54 sponge finger biscuits
cocoa powder, for dusting

method

1 Whip the cream until it just holds its shape. Beat the mascarpone to soften slightly, then fold in the whipped cream. Melt the chocolate in a heatproof bowl set over a saucepan of simmering water, stirring occasionally. Let the chocolate cool slightly, then stir it into the mascarpone and cream mixture.

2 Mix the hot coffee and sugar in a saucepan and stir until dissolved. Leave to cool then add the dark rum. Dip the sponge finger biscuits into the mixture briefly so that they absorb some coffee and rum mixture but do not become soggy.

3 Place 3 sponge finger biscuits on each of 6 serving plates. Spoon a layer of the chocolate, mascarpone and cream mixture over the sponge finger biscuits.

4 Place 3 more sponge finger biscuits on top of the chocolate mixture on each plate. Spread another layer of chocolate mixture and place 3 more sponge finger biscuits on top.

5 Leave to chill in the refrigerator for at least 1 hour. Dust with a little cocoa powder just before serving.

chocolate & cherry tiramisù

ingredients

serves 4

200 ml/7 fl oz strong black coffee,
    cooled to room temperature
90 ml/3 fl oz cherry brandy
16 trifle sponges
250 g/9 oz mascarpone cheese
300 ml/10 fl oz double cream,
    lightly whipped
3 tbsp icing sugar
275 g/9½ oz sweet cherries,
    halved and stoned

to decorate

chocolate curls
whole cherries

method

1 Pour the cooled coffee into a jug and stir in the cherry brandy. Put half of the trifle sponges into a serving dish, then pour over half of the coffee mixture.

2 Put the mascarpone into a separate bowl along with the cream and sugar, and mix well. Spread half of the mascarpone mixture over the coffee-soaked trifle sponges, then top with half of the cherries. Arrange the remaining trifle sponges on top. Pour over the remaining coffee mixture and top with the remaining cherries. Finish with a layer of mascarpone mixture. Scatter over the grated chocolate, cover with clingfilm and chill in the refrigerator for at least 2 hours.

3 Remove from the refrigerator, decorate with the chocolate and cherries, and serve.

marbled chocolate & orange ice cream

ingredients

serves 6

1 tsp cornflour
1 tsp vanilla extract
3 egg yolks
300 ml/10 fl oz milk
175 g/6 oz white chocolate,
    chopped into small pieces
450 ml/16 fl oz double cream
115 g/4 oz orange-flavoured plain
    chocolate, broken into pieces
thinly pared orange rind,
    to decorate
orange segments, to serve

method

1 Beat the cornflour, vanilla extract and egg yolks in a heatproof bowl until well blended. Pour the milk into a large, heavy-based saucepan and bring to the boil over low heat. Pour the milk over the egg yolk mixture, stirring constantly.

2 Strain the mixture back into the pan and heat gently, stirring constantly, until thickened. Remove from the heat, add the white chocolate pieces and stir until melted. Stir in the cream. Set aside 150 ml/5 fl oz of the mixture and pour the remainder into a large freezerproof container. Cover and freeze for 2 hours, or until starting to set. Melt the orange-flavoured chocolate, stir into the reserved mixture and set aside.

3 Remove the partially frozen ice cream from the freezer and beat with a fork. Place spoonfuls of the orange chocolate mixture over the ice cream and swirl with a knife to give a marbled effect. Freeze for 8 hours, or overnight, until firm. Transfer to the refrigerator 30 minutes before serving. Scoop into individual glasses, decorate with orange rind and serve with a few orange segments.

rich chocolate ice cream

ingredients

serves 6

1 egg
3 egg yolks
85 g/3 oz caster sugar
300 ml/10 fl oz whole milk
250 g/9 oz plain chocolate
300 ml/10 fl oz double cream

trellis cups

100 g/3½ oz plain chocolate

method

1 Beat the egg, egg yolks and caster sugar together in a mixing bowl until well combined. Heat the milk until it is almost boiling, then gradually pour it onto the eggs, whisking. Place the bowl over a saucepan of gently simmering water and cook, stirring constantly, until the custard mixture thickens sufficiently to thinly coat the back of a wooden spoon.

2 Break the chocolate into small pieces and add to the hot custard. Stir until the chocolate has melted. Cover and leave to cool.

3 Whip the cream until just holding its shape, then fold into the cooled chocolate custard. Transfer to a freezerproof container and freeze for 1–2 hours until the mixture is frozen 2.5 cm/1 inch from the sides. Scrape the ice cream into a chilled bowl and beat again until smooth. Re-freeze until firm.

4 To make the trellis cups, invert a muffin pan and cover 6 alternate mounds with clingfilm. Melt the chocolate, place it in a paper piping bag, and snip off the end.

5 Pipe a circle around the bottom of the mound, then pipe chocolate back and forth over it to form a double-thickness trellis. Pipe around the bottom again. Chill until set, then lift from the pan and remove the clingfilm. Serve the ice cream in the trellis cups.

coconut & white chocolate ice cream

serves 6

2 eggs
2 egg yolks
115 g/4 oz golden caster sugar
300 ml/10 fl oz single cream
115 g/4 oz white chocolate, chopped
115 g/4 oz creamed coconut, chopped
300 ml/10 fl oz double cream
3 tbsp coconut rum
tropical fruit, such as mango, pineapple or passion fruit, to serve

method

1 Place the whole eggs, egg yolks and sugar in a heatproof bowl and beat together until well blended. Place the single cream, chocolate and coconut in a saucepan and heat gently until the chocolate has melted, then continue to heat, stirring constantly, until almost boiling. Pour onto the egg mixture, stirring vigorously, then set the bowl over a saucepan of gently simmering water, making sure that the base of the bowl does not touch the water.

2 Heat the mixture, stirring constantly, until it lightly coats the back of the spoon. Strain the mixture into a clean, heatproof bowl and allow it to cool. Place the double cream and rum in a separate bowl and whip until slightly thickened, then fold into the cooled chocolate mixture.

3 Freeze the ice cream in an ice cream maker, following the manufacturer's instructions. Transfer to the refrigerator for 30 minutes before serving. Scoop into small serving bowls and serve with tropical fruit.

white chocolate ice cream

ingredients

serves 6

1 egg, plus 1 extra egg yolk
3 tbsp caster sugar
150 g/5½ oz white chocolate
300 ml/10 fl oz milk
150 ml/5 fl oz double cream
plain chocolate, melted, to serve

biscuit cups

1 egg white
55 g/2 oz caster sugar
2 tbsp plain flour, sifted
2 tbsp cocoa powder, sifted
25 g/1 oz butter, melted

method

1 To make the ice cream, beat the egg, egg yolk and sugar together. Break the chocolate into pieces, place in a bowl with 3 tablespoons of milk, and melt over a saucepan of hot water. Heat the milk until almost boiling and pour onto the eggs, whisking. Place over a pan of simmering water and stir until the mixture thickens. Whisk in the chocolate. Cover with dampened baking parchment and let cool.

2 Whip the cream and fold into the custard. Transfer to a freezerproof container and freeze the mixture for 1–2 hours. Scrape into a bowl and beat until smooth. Re-freeze until firm.

3 Line 2 baking sheets with baking parchment. To make the biscuit cups, beat the egg white and sugar. Beat in the flour and cocoa powder, then the butter. Place 1 tablespoon on a baking sheet and spread out into a 13-cm/5-inch circle. Bake in a preheated oven, 200°C/400°F/Gas Mark 6, for 4–5 minutes. Remove and mould over an upturned cup. Let it set, then cool. Repeat to make 6 biscuit cups. Serve the ice cream in the biscuit cups, drizzled with melted chocolate.

sicilian cassata

ingredients

serves 8

150 g/5½ oz self-raising flour
2 tbsp cocoa powder
1 tsp baking powder
175 g/6 oz butter, softened,
    plus extra for greasing
175 g/6 oz golden caster sugar
3 eggs
icing sugar, for dusting
chocolate curls, to decorate

filling

450 g/1 lb ricotta cheese
100 g/3½ oz plain chocolate,
    grated
115 g/4 oz golden caster sugar
3 tbsp Marsala wine
55 g/2 oz chopped candied peel
2 tbsp almonds, chopped

method

1 Grease and base-line a 18-cm/7-inch loose-based round cake tin. Sift the flour, cocoa powder and baking powder into a food processor. Add the butter, sugar and eggs and process thoroughly until smooth and creamy. Pour the cake mixture into the prepared tin and bake in a preheated oven, 190°C/375°F/Gas Mark 5, for 30–40 minutes, or until well risen and firm to the touch. Leave to stand in the tin for 5 minutes, then turn out onto a wire rack to cool completely.

2 Wash and dry the cake tin and grease and line it again. To make the filling, rub the ricotta through a sieve into a bowl. Add the grated chocolate, sugar and Marsala wine and beat together until the mixture is light and fluffy. Stir in the candied peel and almonds.

3 Cut the thin crust off the top of the cake and discard. Cut the cake horizontally into three layers. Place the first slice in the prepared tin and cover with half the ricotta mixture. Repeat the layers, finishing with a cake layer. Press down lightly, cover with a plate and a weight, and chill in the refrigerator for 8 hours, or overnight. To serve, turn the cake out onto a serving plate. Dust with icing sugar and decorate with chocolate curls.

champagne mousses

ingredients

serves 4

sponge

4 eggs
100 g/3½ oz caster sugar
75 g/2¾ oz self-raising flour
2 tbsp cocoa powder
25 g/1 oz butter, melted,
　plus extra for greasing

mousse

1 sachet powdered gelatine
3 tbsp water
300 ml/10 fl oz champagne
300 ml/10 fl oz double cream
2 egg whites
85 g/3 oz caster sugar
50 g/2 oz plain chocolate-
　flavoured cake covering,
　melted, to decorate

method

1 Line a 38 x 25-cm/15 x 10-inch Swiss roll tin with greased baking parchment. Whisk the eggs and sugar with an electric mixer until the mixture is very thick and the whisk leaves a trail when lifted. Sieve the flour and cocoa together and fold into the egg mixture. Fold in the butter. Pour into the prepared tin and bake in a preheated oven, 200°C/400°F/Gas Mark 6, for 8 minutes, or until springy to the touch. Cool in the tin for 5 minutes, then turn out onto a wire rack until cold. Meanwhile, line 4 x 10-cm/4-inch baking rings with baking parchment. Line the sides with 2.5-cm/1-inch strips of cake and the bottom with circles.

2 For the mousse, sprinkle the gelatine over the water and let it go spongy. Place the bowl over a saucepan of hot water and stir until the gelatine has dissolved. Stir in the champagne.

3 Whip the cream until just holding its shape. Fold in the champagne mixture. Stand in a cool place until on the point of setting, stirring. Whisk the egg whites until standing in soft peaks, add the sugar and whisk until glossy. Fold the egg whites into the champagne mixture Spoon into the sponge cases, allowing the mixture to go above the sponge. Chill in the refrigerator for 2 hours. Pipe the chocolate squiggles on a piece of parchment, allow them to set, then use to decorate the mousses.

white chocolate moulds

ingredients

serves 6

125 g/4½ oz white chocolate,
    broken into pieces
250 ml/9 fl oz double cream
3 tbsp crème fraîche
2 eggs, separated
3 tbsp water
1½ tsp powdered gelatine
oil, for brushing
140 g/5 oz sliced strawberries
140 g/5 oz raspberries
140 g/5 oz blackcurrants
70 g/2½ oz caster sugar
125 ml/4 fl oz crème de framboise
12 blackcurrant leaves,
    if available, to decorate

method

1 Put the chocolate in a heatproof bowl set over a saucepan of barely simmering water. Stir over a low heat until melted. Remove from the heat and set aside.

2 Pour the cream into a saucepan and bring to just below boiling point over low heat. Remove from the heat, then stir the cream and crème fraîche into the chocolate and allow to cool slightly. Beat in the egg yolks, one at a time.

3 Pour the water into a bowl and sprinkle over the gelatine. Leave for 2–3 minutes to soften, then set over a saucepan of simmering water until dissolved. Stir into the chocolate mixture and set aside until nearly set.

4 Brush the insides of six timbales or ramekins with oil and line the bases with baking parchment. Whisk the egg whites until soft peaks form, then fold them into the chocolate mixture. Divide the mixture between the moulds and smooth the surface. Cover with clingfilm and chill for 2 hours, until set.

5 Put the strawberries, raspberries and blackcurrants in a bowl. Sprinkle with the caster sugar, then gently stir in the liqueur. Cover with clingfilm and chill for 2 hours.

6 To serve, turn out onto individual plates. Divide the fruit between them and decorate with blackcurrant leaves.

chocolate & orange pots

ingredients

serves 8

200 g/7 oz plain chocolate,
    broken into pieces
grated rind of 1 orange
300 ml/10 fl oz double cream
140 g/5 oz golden caster sugar
3 tbsp Cointreau
3 large egg whites
fine strips of orange rind,
    to decorate
crisp biscuits, to serve

method

1 Melt the chocolate and stir in the orange rind. Place the cream in a bowl with 100 g/3½ oz of the sugar and the Cointreau and whip until thick.

2 Place the egg whites in a clean and grease-free bowl and whisk until soft peaks form, then gradually whisk in the remaining sugar until stiff but not dry. Fold the melted chocolate into the cream, then beat in a spoonful of the whisked egg whites. Gently fold in the remaining egg whites until thoroughly mixed.

3 Spoon the mixture into eight small ramekin dishes or demi-tasse coffee cups. Cover and chill in the refrigerator for 1 hour, then decorate with a few strips of orange rind before serving with crisp biscuits.

coffee panna cotta with chocolate sauce

ingredients

serves 6

oil, for brushing
600 ml/1 pint double cream
1 vanilla pod
55 g/2 oz golden caster sugar
2 tsp instant espresso coffee
    granules, dissolved in
    60 ml/2 fl oz water
2 tsp powdered gelatine

sauce

150 ml/5 fl oz single cream
55 g/2 oz plain chocolate, melted

to decorate

chocolate-covered coffee beans
cocoa, for dusting

method

1 Lightly brush 6 x 150-ml/5-fl oz moulds with oil. Place the cream in a saucepan. Split the vanilla pod and scrape the black seeds into the cream. Add the vanilla pod and the sugar, then heat gently until almost boiling. Sieve the cream into a heatproof bowl and reserve. Place the coffee in a small heatproof bowl, sprinkle on the gelatine and leave for 5 minutes, or until spongy. Set the bowl over a saucepan of gently simmering water until the gelatine has dissolved.

2 Stir a little of the reserved cream into the gelatine mixture, then stir the gelatine mixture into the remainder of the cream. Divide the mixture between the prepared moulds and cool, then chill in the refrigerator for 8 hours, or overnight.

3 To make the sauce, place one quarter of the cream in a bowl and stir in the melted chocolate. Gradually stir in the remaining cream, reserving 1 tablespoon. To serve the panna cotta, dip the bases of the moulds briefly into hot water and turn out onto six dessert plates. Pour the chocolate cream around. Dot drops of the reserved cream onto the sauce and feather it with a skewer. Decorate with chocolate-covered coffee beans and cocoa. Serve immediately.

chocolate marquise

ingredients

serves 6

200 g/7 oz plain chocolate
100 g/3½ oz butter
3 egg yolks
75 g/2¾ oz caster sugar
1 tsp chocolate extract or
    1 tbsp chocolate-flavoured
    liqueur
300 ml/10 fl oz double cream

to serve

chocolate-dipped fruits
crème fraîche
cocoa powder, for dusting

method

1 Break the chocolate into pieces. Place the chocolate and butter in a bowl set over a saucepan of gently simmering water and stir until melted and well combined. Remove the pan from the heat and let the chocolate cool.

2 Place the egg yolks in a mixing bowl with the sugar and whisk until pale and fluffy. Using an electric mixer running on low speed, slowly whisk in the cool chocolate mixture. Stir in the chocolate extract or chocolate-flavoured liqueur.

3 Whip the cream until just holding its shape. Fold into the chocolate mixture. Spoon into 6 small custard pots or individual metal moulds. Chill the desserts in the refrigerator for at least 2 hours.

4 To serve, turn out the desserts onto individual serving dishes. If you have difficulty turning them out, first dip the pots or moulds into a bowl of warm water for a few seconds. Serve with chocolate-dipped fruits and crème fraîche and dust with cocoa.

irish cream cheesecake

ingredients

serves 12

oil, for brushing
175 g/6 oz chocolate chip cookies
55 g/2 oz butter

filling

225 g/8 oz plain chocolate,
    broken into pieces
225 g/8 oz milk chocolate,
    broken into pieces
55 g/2 oz golden caster sugar
350 g/12 oz cream cheese
425 ml/15 fl oz double cream,
    whipped
3 tbsp Irish cream liqueur

to serve

crème fraîche or soured cream
fresh fruit

method

1 Line the base of a 20-cm/8-inch springform tin with foil and brush the sides with oil.

2 Place the cookies in a polythene bag and crush with a rolling pin. Place the butter in a saucepan and heat gently until just melted, then stir in the crushed cookies. Press the mixture into the base of the tin and chill in the refrigerator for 1 hour.

3 To make the filling, melt the plain and milk chocolate together, stir to combine and leave to cool. Place the sugar and cream cheese in a large bowl and beat together until smooth, then fold in the whipped cream. Fold the mixture gently into the melted chocolate, then stir in the Irish cream liqueur.

4 Spoon the filling over the chilled biscuit base and smooth the surface. Cover and chill in the refrigerator for 2 hours, or until quite firm. Transfer to a serving plate and cut into small slices. Serve with a spoonful of crème fraîche and fresh fruit.

chocolate terrine with orange cream

ingredients

serves 10–12

90 ml/3 fl oz water
3 tsp powdered gelatine
115 g/4 oz each of milk, white
   and plain chocolate, broken
   into pieces
450 ml/16 fl oz whipping cream
6 eggs, separated
75 g/2¼ oz caster sugar

orange cream

2 tbsp caster sugar
1 tbsp cornflour
2 egg yolks
150 ml/5 fl oz milk
150 ml/5 fl oz double cream
grated rind of 1 orange
1 tbsp Cointreau

to decorate

150 ml/5 fl oz double cream,
   whipped
chocolate-covered coffee beans
orange zest

method

1 To make the milk chocolate mousse, place 2 tablespoons of the water in a heatproof bowl. Sprinkle on 1 teaspoon of gelatine and stand for 5 minutes. Set the bowl over a saucepan of simmering water until the gelatine has dissolved. Leave to cool. Melt the milk chocolate and let it cool. Whip one-third of the cream until thick. Whisk two of the egg whites in a bowl until stiff but not dry. Whisk two of the egg yolks and one third of the sugar in a separate bowl until thick. Stir in the chocolate, gelatine and whipped cream. Fold in the egg whites.

2 Line a 1.2-litre/2¾-pint loaf tin with clingfilm. Pour in the mixture. Cover and freeze for 20 minutes. Make the white chocolate mousse in the same way, pour over the milk chocolate mousse and freeze. Make the plain chocolate mousse and pour on top. Chill for 2 hours.

3 To make the orange cream, stir the sugar, cornflour and egg yolks together until smooth. Heat the milk, cream and orange rind in a saucepan until almost boiling, then pour over the egg mixture, whisking. Strain back into the pan and heat until thick. Cover and cool, then stir in the Cointreau. Turn out the terrine and decorate with cream, beans and zest. Serve with the orange cream.

cakes & tortes

chocolate brownie cake

ingredients

serves 10

200 g/7 oz butter,
    plus extra for greasing
115 g/4 oz plain chocolate,
    broken into pieces
280 g/10 oz granulated sugar
115 g/4 oz light muscovado sugar
4 eggs, beaten
175 g/6 oz plain flour
1 tsp vanilla extract
pinch of salt
75 g/2³/₄ oz dried cranberries
75 g/2³/₄ oz toasted flaked
    almonds, plus extra to decorate

icing

115 g/4 oz plain chocolate
25 g/1 oz butter
225 g/8 oz icing sugar
60 ml/2 fl oz milk

method

1 Grease and line the bases of 2 x 18-cm/7-inch round shallow cake tins with baking parchment.

2 Place the butter in a heavy-based saucepan and add the chocolate. Heat gently, stirring frequently until the mixture has melted. Remove from the heat and stir until smooth. Add the sugars, stir well, then leave to cool for 10 minutes.

3 Gradually add the eggs to the cooled chocolate mixture, beating well after each addition. Stir in the flour, vanilla extract and salt. Stir in the cranberries and flaked almonds, mix, then divide between the prepared cake tins.

4 Bake in a preheated oven,180°C/350°F/Gas Mark 4, for 25–30 minutes, or until springy to the touch. Remove from the oven and leave to cool. Turn out onto a wire rack and leave until cold.

5 To make the icing, melt the chocolate and butter in a saucepan and stir until smooth. Gradually beat in the icing sugar with enough milk to give a smooth spreading consistency. Use the icing to sandwich the two cakes together, then spread the top and sides with the remainder, swirling the top to give a decorative effect. Sprinkle the flaked almonds over the top to decorate. Let the icing set before serving the cake.

dark & white fudge cupcakes

ingredients

makes 20

200 ml/7 fl oz water
85 g/3 oz butter
85 g/3 oz caster sugar
1 tbsp golden syrup
3 tbsp milk
1 tsp vanilla extract
1 tsp bicarbonate of soda
225 g/8 oz plain flour
2 tbsp cocoa powder

icing

50 g/1¾ oz plain chocolate
60 ml/2 fl oz water
50 g/1¾ oz butter
50 g/1¾ oz white chocolate
350 g/12 oz icing sugar

to decorate

100 g/3½ oz plain chocolate
  shavings
100 g/3½ oz white chocolate
  shavings

method

1 Put 20 paper baking cases in 2 bun trays, or put 20 double-layer paper cases on 2 baking trays.

2 Put the water, butter, sugar and syrup in a saucepan. Heat gently, stirring, until the sugar has dissolved, then bring to the boil. Reduce the heat and cook gently for 5 minutes. Remove from the heat and leave to cool.

3 Meanwhile, put the milk and vanilla extract in a bowl. Add the bicarbonate of soda and stir to dissolve. Sift the flour and cocoa powder into a separate bowl and add the syrup mixture. Stir in the milk and beat until smooth. Spoon the mixture into the paper cases until they are two-thirds full.

4 Bake the cupcakes in a preheated oven, 180°C/350°F/ Gas Mark 4, for 20 minutes, or until well risen and firm to the touch. Transfer to a wire rack and leave to cool.

5 To make the icing, break the plain chocolate into a small heatproof bowl, add half the water and half the butter, and set the bowl over a saucepan of gently simmering water until melted. Stir until smooth and leave to stand over the water. Repeat with the white chocolate and remaining water and butter. Sift half the icing sugar into each bowl and beat until smooth and thick. Top the cupcakes with the icing then leave to set. Serve decorated with chocolate shavings.

blackberry chocolate flan

ingredients

serves 6

pastry

140 g/5 oz plain flour, plus extra
    for dusting
25 g/1 oz cocoa powder
55 g/2 oz icing sugar
pinch of salt
85 g/3 oz butter, cut into
    small pieces
½ egg yolk

filling

300 ml/10 fl oz double cream
175 g/6 oz blackberry jam
225 g/8 oz plain chocolate,
    broken into pieces
25 g/1 oz unsalted butter,
    cut into small pieces

sauce

675 g/1 lb 8 oz blackberries,
    plus extra to decorate
1 tbsp lemon juice
2 tbsp caster sugar
2 tbsp crème de cassis

method

1 To make the pastry, sift the flour, cocoa powder, icing sugar and salt into a food processor. Add the butter and egg yolk and gradually mix in the dry ingredients. Knead lightly and form into a ball. Wrap the dough in clingfilm and chill in the refrigerator for 1 hour.

2 Roll out the pastry on a lightly floured work surface. Use it to line a 30 x 10-cm/12 x 4-inch rectangular flan tin and prick the pastry case with a fork. Line the base with greaseproof paper and fill with baking beans. Bake in a preheated oven, 180°C/350°F/Gas Mark 4, for 15 minutes. Take out of the oven and remove the paper and beans. Set aside to cool.

3 To make the filling, put the cream and jam in a saucepan and bring to the boil over a low heat. Remove the saucepan from the heat and stir in the chocolate and then the butter until melted and smooth. Pour the mixture into the pastry case and set aside to cool.

4 To make the sauce, put the blackberries, lemon juice and caster sugar in a food processor and process until smooth. Strain through a nylon sieve into a bowl and stir in the cassis. Set aside. Remove the flan from the tin and place on a serving plate. Arrange the blackberries on top and brush with the blackberry and liqueur sauce. Serve the flan with the remaining sauce on the side.

devil's food cake

ingredients

serves 10–12

100 g/3½ oz plain chocolate,
broken into pieces
250 g/9 oz self-raising flour
1 tsp bicarbonate of soda
225 g/8 oz butter, plus extra
for greasing
400 g/14 oz dark brown sugar
1 tsp vanilla extract
3 eggs
125 ml/4 fl oz buttermilk
225 ml/8 fl oz boiling water

frosting

300 g/10½ oz caster sugar
2 egg whites
1 tbsp lemon juice
3 tbsp orange juice
candied orange peel, to decorate

method

1 Lightly grease and base-line 2 x 20-cm/8-inch shallow round cake tins.

2 Melt the chocolate in a heatproof bowl over a saucepan of simmering water. Sift the flour and bicarbonate of soda together.

3 Place the butter and sugar in a large bowl and beat until pale and fluffy. Beat in the vanilla extract and the eggs, one at a time, beating well after each addition. Add a little flour if the mixture starts to curdle. Fold the melted chocolate into the mixture until well blended. Fold in the remaining flour, then stir in the buttermilk and the boiling water.

4 Divide the mixture between the prepared tins. Bake in a preheated oven, 190°C/375°F/Gas Mark 5, for 30 minutes, or until springy to the touch. Cool in the pan for 5 minutes, then transfer to a wire rack to cool.

5 Place the frosting ingredients in a large bowl set over a pan of simmering water. Using an electric whisk, whisk until thick and forming soft peaks. Remove from the heat and whisk until the mixture is cool.

6 Sandwich the two cakes together with a little of the frosting, then spread the remainder over the sides and top of the cake. Decorate with candied orange peel.

mocha layer cake

ingredients

serves 8

butter, for greasing
200 g/7 oz self-raising flour
¼ tsp baking powder
4 tbsp cocoa powder
100 g/3½ oz caster sugar
2 eggs
2 tbsp golden syrup
150 ml/5 fl oz corn oil
150 ml/5 fl oz milk

filling

1 tsp instant coffee
1 tbsp boiling water
300 ml/10 fl oz double cream
2 tbsp icing sugar

to decorate

50 g/1¾ oz plain chocolate, grated
chocolate caraque
icing sugar, for dusting

method

1 Lightly grease 3 x 18-cm/7-inch shallow round cake tins. Sift the flour, baking powder and cocoa into a large bowl, then stir in the sugar. Make a well in the centre and stir in the eggs, syrup, corn oil and milk. Beat with a wooden spoon, gradually mixing in the dry ingredients to make a smooth mixture. Divide the mixture between the prepared tins.

2 Bake in a preheated oven, 180°C/350°F/Gas Mark 4, for 35–45 minutes, or until springy to the touch. Cool in the tins for 5 minutes, then turn out and cool completely on a wire rack.

3 To make the filling, dissolve the instant coffee in the boiling water and place in a large bowl with the cream and icing sugar. Whip until the cream is just holding its shape, then use half the cream to sandwich the three cakes together. Spread the remaining cream over the top and sides of the cake. Press the grated chocolate into the cream round the edge of the cake.

4 Transfer the cake to a serving plate. Lay the chocolate caraque over the top of the cake. Cut a few thin strips of baking parchment and place on top of the chocolate caraque. Dust lightly with icing sugar, then carefully remove the parchment. Serve.

chocolate ganache cake

ingredients

serves 10

175 g/6 oz butter, plus extra
    for greasing
175 g/6 oz caster sugar
4 eggs, lightly beaten
200 g/7 oz self-raising flour
1 tbsp cocoa powder
50 g/1¾ oz plain chocolate,
    melted

ganache

450 ml/16 fl oz double cream
375 g/13 oz plain chocolate,
    broken into pieces
200 g/7 oz chocolate-flavoured
    cake covering, to finish

method

1 Lightly grease and base-line a 20-cm/8-inch springform
   cake tin. Beat the butter and sugar until light and fluffy.
   Gradually add the eggs, beating well. Sift the flour and
   cocoa together. Fold into the cake mixture. Fold in the
   melted chocolate. Pour the mixture into the prepared
   tin and smooth the top.

2 Bake in a preheated oven, 180°C/350°F/Gas Mark 4,
   for 40 minutes, or until springy to the touch. Cool for
   5 minutes in the tin, then turn out onto a wire rack to
   cool completely. Cut the cold cake into two layers.

3 To make the ganache, place the cream in a saucepan
   and bring to the boil, stirring. Add the chocolate and
   stir until melted and combined. Pour into a bowl
   and whisk for about 5 minutes or until fluffy and cool.
   Set aside one third of the ganache and use the rest to
   sandwich the cake together and spread smoothly and
   evenly over the top and sides of the cake.

4 Melt the cake covering and spread it over a large sheet
   of baking parchment. Cool until just set. Cut into strips
   a little wider than the height of the cake. Place them
   around the edge of the cake, overlapping slightly.

5 Using a piping bag with a fine nozzle, pipe the reserved
   ganache in tear drops or shells to cover the top of the
   cake. Chill for 1 hour in the refrigerator before serving.

white truffle cake

ingredients

serves 12

butter, for greasing
2 eggs
55 g/2 oz caster sugar
55 g/2 oz plain flour
50 g/1¼ oz white chocolate,
    melted

truffle topping

300 ml/10 fl oz double cream
350 g/12 oz white chocolate,
    broken into pieces
250 g/9 oz mascarpone cheese

to decorate

plain, milk or white chocolate
    caraque
cocoa powder, for dusting

method

1 Grease and line a 20-cm/8-inch round springform cake tin. Whisk the eggs and caster sugar in a mixing bowl for 10 minutes or until the mixture is very light and foamy and the whisk leaves a trail that lasts a few seconds when lifted. Sift the flour and fold in with a metal spoon. Fold in the melted white chocolate.

2 Pour into the prepared tin and bake in a preheated oven, 180°C/350°F/Gas Mark 4, for 25 minutes, or until springy to the touch. Cool slightly in the tin, then transfer to a wire rack to cool completely. Wash and dry the cake tin and return the cold cake to the tin, again lined and greased.

3 To make the topping, place the cream in a pan and bring to the boil, stirring to prevent it sticking to the bottom of the pan. Cool slightly, then add the white chocolate pieces and stir until melted and combined. Remove from the heat and stir until almost cool, then stir in the mascarpone cheese. Pour the mixture on top of the cake and chill in the refrigerator for 2 hours.

4 Transfer the cake to a plate. Decorate the top of the cake with the caraque. Dust with cocoa powder. Serve.

double chocolate gâteau

ingredients

serves 10

filling
250 ml/9 fl oz whipping cream
225 g/8 oz white chocolate, broken
    into pieces

sponge
225 g/8 oz butter, softened,
    plus extra for greasing
225 g/8 oz golden caster sugar
4 eggs, beaten
175 g/6 oz self-raising flour
55 g/2 oz cocoa powder

frosting
350 g/12 oz plain chocolate,
    broken into pieces
115 g/4 oz butter
85 ml/3 fl oz double cream

to decorate
grated chocolate or chocolate curls,
    chilled
2 tsp icing sugar and cocoa powder

method

1 To make the filling, heat the cream to almost boiling.
   Place the white chocolate in a food processor and
   chop coarsely. Pour the cream through the feed tube.
   Process for 10–15 seconds, or until the mixture is
   smooth. Transfer to a bowl to cool, then cover and chill
   in the refrigerator for 2 hours, or until firm to the touch.
   Whisk the mixture until just starting to hold soft peaks.

2 Grease and base-line a 20-cm/8-inch deep round cake
   tin. To make the sponge, beat the butter and sugar
   together until light and fluffy. Gradually beat in the
   eggs. Sift the flour and cocoa into another bowl,
   then fold into the mixture. Spoon the mixture into the
   prepared tin and level the surface. Bake in a preheated
   oven, 180°C/350°F/Gas Mark 4, for 45–50 minutes, or
   until springy to the touch and the tip of a knife inserted
   into the centre comes out clean. Cool in the tin for
   5 minutes, then cool completely on a wire rack.

3 To make the frosting, melt the chocolate. Stir in the
   butter and cream. Cool, stirring frequently, until the
   mixture is a spreading consistency. Slice the cake into
   three layers. Sandwich the layers together with the
   filling. Cover the cake with frosting and put grated
   chocolate or curls on top. Mix together the icing sugar
   and cocoa and sift over the cake. Serve.

double chocolate roulade

ingredients

serves 8

4 eggs, separated
115 g/4 oz golden caster sugar
115 g/4 oz plain chocolate,
    melted and cooled
1 tsp instant coffee granules,
    dissolved in 2 tbsp hot water,
    cooled
icing sugar, to decorate
cocoa powder, for dusting
fresh raspberries, to serve

filling

250 ml/9 fl oz whipping cream
140 g/5 oz white chocolate,
    broken into pieces
3 tbsp Tia Maria

method

1 Line a 23 x 33-cm/9 x 13-inch Swiss roll pan with
  baking parchment. Whisk the egg yolks and sugar in a
  bowl until pale and mousse-like. Fold in the chocolate,
  then the coffee. Place the egg whites in a clean bowl
  and whisk until stiff but not dry. Stir a little of the egg
  whites into the chocolate mixture, then fold in the
  remainder. Pour into the pan and bake in a preheated
  oven, 180°C/350°F/Gas Mark 4, for 15–20 minutes, or
  until firm to the touch. Cover the tin with a damp tea
  towel and set aside for 8 hours, or overnight.

2 Meanwhile, make the filling. Heat the cream until
  almost boiling. Place the chocolate in a food processor
  and chop coarsely. With the motor running, pour the
  cream through the feed tube. Process until smooth.
  Stir in the Tia Maria. Transfer to a bowl and cool, then
  chill in the refrigerator for 8 hours, or overnight.

3 To assemble the roulade, whip the chocolate cream
  until soft peaks form. Cut a sheet of waxed paper larger
  than the roulade, place on a work surface and sift icing
  sugar over it. Turn the roulade out onto the paper.
  Peel away the lining paper. Spread the chocolate cream
  over the roulade and roll up from the short side nearest
  to you. Transfer to a dish, seam-side down. Chill for
  2 hours in the refrigerator, then dust with cocoa. Serve
  with raspberries.

chocolate & orange cake

ingredients

serves 8

175 g/6 oz caster sugar
175 g/6 oz butter, plus extra
    for greasing
3 eggs, beaten
175 g/6 oz self-raising flour, sifted
2 tbsp cocoa powder, sifted
2 tbsp milk
3 tbsp orange juice
grated rind of ½ orange

frosting

175 g/6 oz icing sugar
2 tbsp orange juice
a little melted chocolate

method

1 Lightly grease a 20-cm/8-inch deep round cake tin.
   Beat the sugar and butter together in a bowl until light
   and fluffy. Gradually add the eggs, beating well after
   each addition. Carefully fold in the flour. Divide the
   mixture in half. Add the cocoa and milk to one half,
   until well combined. Flavour the other half with the
   orange juice and grated orange rind.

2 Place spoonfuls of each mixture into the prepared tin
   and swirl together with a skewer, to create a marbled
   effect. Bake in a preheated oven, 190°C/375°F/Gas
   Mark 5, for 25 minutes, or until the cake is springy to
   the touch. Cool in the tin for a few minutes before
   transferring to a wire rack to cool completely.

3 To make the frosting, sift the icing sugar into a mixing
   bowl and mix in enough of the orange juice to form a
   smooth frosting. Spread the frosting over the top of
   the cake and leave to set. Pipe fine lines of melted
   chocolate over the top, then drag a cocktail stick in the
   opposite direction to create a feathered effect. Serve.

date & chocolate cake

ingredients

serves 6

115 g/4 oz plain chocolate
1 tbsp grenadine
1 tbsp golden syrup
115 g/4 oz unsalted butter,
     plus extra for greasing
55 g/2 oz caster sugar
2 large eggs
85 g/3 oz self-raising flour,
     plus extra for dusting
2 tbsp ground rice
1 tbsp icing sugar, to decorate

filling

115 g/4 oz dried dates, chopped
1 tbsp orange juice
1 tbsp demerara sugar
25 g/1 oz blanched almonds,
     chopped
2 tbsp apricot jam

method

1 Grease 2 x 18-cm/7-inch sandwich tins, and dust with flour.

2 Break the chocolate into pieces, then place the chocolate, grenadine and syrup in the top of a double boiler or in a heatproof bowl set over a pan of barely simmering water. Stir over low heat until the chocolate has melted and the mixture is smooth. Remove the pan from the heat and set aside to cool.

3 Beat the butter and caster sugar together in a bowl until pale and fluffy. Gradually beat in the eggs, then beat in the chocolate mixture. Sift the flour into another bowl and stir in the ground rice. Fold the 2 mixtures together.

4 Divide the cake mixture between the prepared tins and level the surfaces. Bake in a preheated oven, 180°C/350°F/Gas Mark 4, for 20–25 minutes, or until golden and firm to the touch. Turn out onto a wire rack to cool.

5 To make the filling, put all the ingredients into a saucepan and stir over low heat for 4–5 minutes, or until fully blended. Remove from the heat, allow to cool, then use the filling to sandwich the cakes together. Dust the top of the cake with icing sugar and serve.

chocolate marshmallow cake

ingredients

serves 6

6 tbsp unsalted butter, plus
    extra for greasing
225 g/8 oz caster sugar
½ tsp vanilla extract
2 eggs, lightly beaten
85 g/3 oz plain chocolate,
    broken into pieces
150 ml/5 fl oz buttermilk
175 g/6 oz self-raising flour
½ tsp bicarbonate of soda
pinch of salt

frosting

175 g/6 oz white marshmallows
1 tbsp milk
2 egg whites
2 tbsp caster sugar
55 g/2 oz milk chocolate, grated,
    to decorate

method

1 Grease a 850-ml/1½-pint ovenproof bowl. Cream the
    butter, sugar and vanilla together in a mixing bowl
    until pale and fluffy, then gradually beat in the eggs.

2 Melt the chocolate in a bowl over a saucepan of
    simmering water. Gradually stir in the buttermilk until
    well combined. Cool slightly.

3 Sift the flour, bicarbonate of soda and salt into a
    separate bowl. Add the chocolate and the flour
    mixtures alternately to the creamed mixture, a little
    at a time. Spoon the mixture into the prepared bowl.
    Bake in a preheated oven, 160°C/325°F/Gas Mark 3,
    for 50 minutes until a skewer inserted into the centre
    of the cake comes out clean. Turn out onto a wire rack
    to cool.

4 Meanwhile, make the frosting. Heat the marshmallows
    and milk very gently in a small saucepan until the
    marshmallows have melted. Remove from the heat
    and cool. Whisk the egg whites until soft peaks form,
    then add the sugar and continue whisking, until stiff
    peaks form. Fold into the cooled marshmallow mixture
    and set aside for 10 minutes.

5 When the cake is cool, cover the top and sides with the
    marshmallow frosting. Top with grated milk chocolate.
    Serve.

family chocolate cake

ingredients

serves 8

125 g/4½ oz soft margarine,
    plus extra for greasing
125 g/4½ oz caster sugar
2 eggs
1 tbsp golden syrup
125 g/4½ oz self-raising
    flour, sifted
2 tbsp cocoa powder, sifted

filling and topping

4 tbsp icing sugar, sifted
25 g/1 oz butter
100 g/3½ oz white or milk
    cooking chocolate
a little milk or white chocolate,
    melted (optional)

method

1 Lightly grease 2 x 18-cm/7-inch shallow cake tins.
   Place all of the ingredients for the cake in a large
   mixing bowl and beat well with a wooden spoon to
   form a smooth mixture.

2 Divide the mixture between the tins and smooth
   the tops. Bake in a preheated oven, 190°C/375°F/Gas
   Mark 5, for 20 minutes or until springy to the touch.
   Cool for a few minutes in the tins, then transfer the
   cakes to a wire rack to cool completely.

3 To make the filling, beat the sugar and butter together
   in a bowl until light and fluffy. Melt the white or milk
   cooking chocolate and beat half into the icing mixture.
   Use the filling to sandwich the two cakes together.

4 Spread the remaining melted cooking chocolate
   over the top of the cake. Pipe circles of contrasting
   milk or white chocolate and feather into the cooking
   chocolate with a cocktail stick, if desired. Allow the
   cake to set before serving.

mocha cupcakes with whipped cream

ingredients

makes 20

2 tbsp instant espresso
   coffee powder
150 g/5½ oz butter
100 g/3½ oz caster sugar
1 tbsp honey
250 ml/8½ fl oz water
225 g/8 oz plain flour
2 tbsp cocoa powder
1 tsp bicarbonate of soda
3 tbsp milk
1 large egg, lightly beaten

topping

225 ml/8 fl oz whipping cream
cocoa powder, sifted,
   for dusting

method

1 Put 20 paper baking cases in 2 muffin tins, or put
   20 double-layer paper cases on 2 baking sheets.

2 Put the coffee powder, butter, sugar, honey and water
   in a saucepan and heat gently, stirring, until the sugar
   has dissolved. Bring to the boil, then reduce the heat
   and simmer for 5 minutes. Pour into a large heatproof
   bowl and set aside to cool.

3 When the mixture has cooled, sift in the flour and
   cocoa. Dissolve the bicarbonate of soda in the milk,
   then add to the mixture with the egg and beat
   together until smooth. Spoon the mixture into the
   paper cases.

4 Bake the cupcakes in a preheated oven, 180°C/350°F/
   Gas Mark 4, for 15–20 minutes, or until well risen and
   firm to the touch. Transfer to a wire rack to cool
   completely.

5 For the topping, whisk the cream in a bowl until it
   holds its shape. Just before serving, spoon heaping
   teaspoonfuls of cream on top of each cake, then dust
   lightly with sifted cocoa. Store the cupcakes in the
   refrigerator until ready to serve.

warm molten-centred chocolate cupcakes

ingredients

makes 8

50 g/2 oz soft margarine
55 g/2 oz caster sugar
1 large egg
85 g/3 oz self-raising flour
1 tbsp cocoa powder
55 g/2 oz plain chocolate
icing sugar, for dusting

method

1 Put 8 paper baking cases in a muffin tin, or place 8 double-layer paper cases on a baking sheet.

2 Put the margarine, sugar, egg, flour and cocoa in a large bowl and, using an electric hand whisk, beat together until just smooth.

3 Spoon half of the mixture into the paper cases. Using a teaspoon, make an indentation in the centre of each cake. Break the chocolate evenly into 8 squares and place a piece in each indentation, then spoon the remaining cake mixture on top.

4 Bake the cupcakes in a preheated oven, 190°C/375°F/ Gas Mark 5, for 20 minutes, or until well risen and springy to the touch. Leave to stand for 2–3 minutes before serving warm, dusted with sifted icing sugar.

dark & white chocolate torte

ingredients

serves 6

butter, for greasing
4 eggs
100 g/3½ oz caster sugar
100 g/3½ oz plain flour

filling

300 ml/10 fl oz double cream
150 g/5½ oz plain chocolate,
    broken into small pieces

topping

75 g/2¾ oz white chocolate
1 tbsp butter
1 tbsp milk
70 g/2½ oz icing sugar
shavings of chocolate, to decorate

method

1 Grease and base-line a 20-cm/8-inch round springform cake tin. Whisk the eggs and caster sugar in a large bowl with an electric whisk for 10 minutes, or until the mixture is very light and foamy and the whisk leaves a trail that lasts a few seconds when lifted.

2 Sift the flour and fold in with a metal spoon or spatula. Pour into the prepared cake tin and bake in a preheated oven, 180°C/350°F/Gas Mark 4, for 35–40 minutes, or until springy to the touch. Cool slightly in the tin, then transfer to a wire rack to cool completely.

3 For the filling, place the cream in a pan and bring to the boil, stirring. Add the chocolate and stir until melted. Remove from the heat, transfer to a bowl, and leave to cool. Beat with a wooden spoon until thick.

4 Slice the cold cake horizontally into two layers. Sandwich the layers together with the plain chocolate cream and place on a wire rack.

5 For the topping, melt the chocolate and butter together and stir until blended. Whisk in the milk and icing sugar. Continue whisking for a few minutes until the frosting is cool. Pour it over the cake and spread with a spatula to coat the top and sides. Allow the frosting to set before serving, decorated with chocolate shavings.

chocolate & almond torte

ingredients

serves 10

225 g/8 oz plain chocolate,
    broken into pieces
3 tbsp water
150 g/5½ oz brown sugar
175 g/6 oz butter, softened,
    plus extra for greasing
25 g/1 oz ground almonds
3 tbsp self-raising flour
5 eggs, separated
100 g/3½ oz finely chopped
    blanched almonds
icing sugar, for dusting
fresh berries and double cream,
    to serve

method

1 Grease and base-line a 23-cm/9-inch loose-based cake tin. Melt the chocolate with the water in a saucepan set over very low heat, stirring until smooth. Add the sugar and stir until dissolved, removing the pan from the heat to prevent it overheating.

2 Add the butter in small amounts until it has melted into the chocolate. Remove from the heat and lightly stir in the ground almonds and flour. Add the egg yolks one at a time, beating well after each addition.

3 Whisk the egg whites in a large mixing bowl, until they stand in soft peaks, then fold them into the chocolate mixture with a metal spoon. Stir in the chopped almonds. Pour the mixture into the prepared tin and smooth the surface.

4 Bake in a preheated oven, 180°C/350°F/Gas Mark 4, for 40–45 minutes, or until well risen and firm to the touch (the cake will crack on the surface during cooking).

5 Cool in the tin for 30–40 minutes, then turn out onto a wire rack to cool completely. Dust with icing sugar and serve in slices with fresh berries and cream.

chocolate truffle torte

ingredients

serves 10

butter, for greasing
55 g/2 oz golden caster sugar
2 eggs
25 g/1 oz plain flour
25 g/1 oz cocoa powder, plus
      extra for decorating
50 ml/2 fl oz cold strong
      black coffee
2 tbsp brandy
icing sugar, to decorate

topping

600 ml/1 pint whipping cream
425 g/15 oz plain chocolate,
      melted and cooled

method

1 Grease and base-line a 23-cm/9-inch springform cake tin. Place the sugar and eggs in a heatproof bowl and set over a saucepan of hot water. Whisk together until pale and mousse-like. Sift the flour and cocoa powder into a separate bowl, then fold gently into the cake mixture. Pour the mixture into the prepared tin and bake in a preheated oven, 220°C/425°F/Gas Mark 7, for 7–10 minutes, or until risen and firm to the touch.

2 Transfer to a wire rack to cool completely. Wash and dry the tin and replace the cake in the tin. Mix the coffee and brandy together and brush over the cake.

3 To make the topping, place the cream in a bowl and whip until very soft peaks form. Carefully fold in the cooled chocolate. Pour the mixture over the sponge. Chill in the refrigerator for 4–5 hours, or until set.

4 To decorate the torte, sift cocoa powder over the top and remove carefully from the tin. Using strips of card or waxed paper as a guide, sift bands of icing sugar over the torte to create a striped pattern. To serve, cut into slices with a hot knife.

biscuits, bars & traybakes

chocolate orange biscuits

ingredients

makes 30

90 g/3¼ oz butter, softened
60 g/2¼ oz caster sugar
1 egg
1 tbsp milk
280 g/10 oz plain flour,
    plus extra for dusting
2 tbsp cocoa powder

icing

175 g/6 oz icing sugar, sifted
3 tbsp orange juice
a little plain chocolate,
    broken into pieces

method

1 Line 2 baking sheets with sheets of baking parchment. Beat together the butter and sugar until the mixture is light and fluffy. Beat in the egg and milk until well combined. Sift the flour and cocoa into the bowl and gradually mix together to form a soft dough. Add the rest of the flour and bring the dough together.

2 Roll out the dough on a lightly floured work surface until 5 mm/¼ inch thick. Cut out circles using a 5-cm/2-inch fluted round biscuit cutter. Place the circles on the prepared baking sheets and bake in a preheated oven, 180°C/350°F/Gas Mark 4, for 10–12 minutes, or until golden. Let the biscuits cool on the baking sheet for a few minutes before peeling them off and transferring them to a wire rack to cool completely and become crisp.

3 To make the icing, put the icing sugar in a bowl and stir in enough orange juice to form a thin icing that will coat the back of the spoon. Put a spoonful of icing in the centre of each biscuit and leave to set. Place the plain chocolate in a heatproof bowl set over a saucepan of gently simmering water and stir until melted. Drizzle thin lines of melted chocolate over the biscuits and leave to set before serving.

viennese fingers

ingredients

makes 16

100 g/3½ oz unsalted butter,
  plus extra for greasing
25 g/1 oz golden caster sugar
½ tsp vanilla extract
100 g/3½ oz self-raising flour
100 g/3½ oz plain chocolate,
  broken into fingers

method

1 Lightly grease 2 baking trays. Place the butter, sugar and vanilla extract in a bowl and cream together until pale and fluffy. Stir in the flour, mixing evenly to a fairly stiff dough.

2 Place the mixture in a piping bag fitted with a large star nozzle and pipe about 16 fingers, each 6 cm/ 2½ inches long, onto the prepared baking trays.

3 Bake in a preheated oven, 160°C/325°F/Gas Mark 3, for 10–15 minutes, until pale golden. Cool for 2–3 minutes on the baking trays, then lift carefully onto a wire rack with a palette knife to cool completely.

4 Place the chocolate in a small heatproof bowl set over a pan of gently simmering water until melted. Remove from the heat. Dip the ends of each biscuit into the chocolate to coat, then place on a sheet of baking paper and leave to set.

variation

Pipe the mixture into a star shapes using a star-shaped mould and bake. Dip the tips into a little melted chocolate.

chocolate pistachio bars

ingredients
makes 24

175 g/6 oz plain chocolate,
    broken into pieces
25 g/1 oz butter, plus extra
    for greasing
350 g/12 oz self-raising flour,
    plus extra for dusting
1½ tsp baking powder
85 g/3 oz caster sugar
70 g/2½ oz polenta
finely grated rind of 1 lemon
2 tsp amaretto
1 egg, lightly beaten
115 g/4 oz pistachio nuts,
    roughly chopped
2 tbsp icing sugar, for dusting

method

1 Lightly grease 2 large baking sheets. Put the chocolate and the butter in a heatproof bowl set over a saucepan of gently simmering water. Stir over a low heat until melted and smooth. Remove from the heat and leave to cool slightly.

2 Sift the flour and baking powder into a bowl and mix in the caster sugar, cornmeal, lemon rind, amaretto, egg and pistachio nuts. Stir in the chocolate mixture and mix to a soft dough.

3 Lightly dust your hands with flour, divide the dough in half and shape each piece into a 28-cm/11-inch long rolls. Transfer the rolls to the prepared baking sheets and flatten, with the palm of your hand, to about 2 cm/¾ inch thick. Bake in a preheated oven, 160°C/325°F/Gas Mark 3, for about 20 minutes, or until firm to the touch.

4 Remove the baking sheet from the oven and leave the rolls to cool. When cool, put the rolls on a chopping board and slice them diagonally into thin biscuits. Return them to the baking sheet and bake for an additional 10 minutes, or until crisp. Remove from the oven and transfer to a wire rack to cool completely. Dust lightly with icing sugar. Serve.

zebra biscuits

ingredients

makes 18–20

55 g/2 oz plain chocolate,
    broken into pieces
140 g/5 oz plain flour
1 tsp baking powder
1 egg
140 g/5 oz caster sugar
50 ml/2 fl oz sunflower oil,
    plus extra for oiling
½ tsp vanilla extract
2 tbsp icing sugar
1 small packet milk chocolate
    buttons
1 small packet white chocolate
    buttons

method

1 Oil 2 large baking sheets. Melt the chocolate in
    a heatproof bowl set over a saucepan of gently
    simmering water. Leave to cool. Sift the flour and
    baking powder together.

2 Meanwhile, in a large bowl, whisk the egg, sugar,
    oil and vanilla extract together. Whisk in the cooled,
    melted chocolate until well blended, then gradually
    stir in the sifted flour. Cover the bowl and leave to chill
    in the refrigerator for at least 3 hours.

3 Using your hands, shape tablespoonfuls of the mixture
    into log shapes, each measuring about 5 cm/2 inches.

4 Roll the logs generously in the icing sugar, then place
    on the prepared baking sheets, allowing room for the
    biscuits to spread during cooking.

5 Bake in a preheated oven, 190°C/375°F/Gas Mark 5, for
    about 15 minutes, or until firm to the touch. As soon as
    the biscuits are done, place 3 chocolate buttons down
    the centre of each, alternating the colours. Transfer to
    a wire rack and leave to cool. Serve.

chocolate chip flapjacks

ingredients

makes 12

115 g/4 oz butter, plus extra
    for greasing
60 g/2¼ oz caster sugar
1 tbsp golden syrup
350 g/12 oz rolled oats
85 g/3 oz plain chocolate chips
85 g/3 oz sultanas

method

1 Lightly grease a 20-cm/8-inch square, shallow cake tin.

2 Place the butter, sugar and syrup in a saucepan and
    cook over a low heat, stirring constantly, until the
    butter and sugar melt and the mixture is well combined.

3 Remove the saucepan from the heat and stir in
    the rolled oats until they are well coated. Add the
    chocolate chips and the sultanas and mix well to
    combine everything.

4 Turn the mixture into the prepared tin and press
    down well.

5 Bake in a preheated oven, 180°C/350°F/Gas Mark 4, for
    30 minutes. Cool slightly, then mark into squares. When
    almost cold, cut into squares and transfer to a wire rack
    to cool completely.

variation

Add 55 g/2 oz of chopped glacé cherries to the flapjacks
at the same time as the chocolate chips and sultanas.

nutty chocolate drizzles

ingredients

makes 24

250 g/9 oz butter or margarine,
    plus extra for greasing
325 g/11½ oz brown sugar
1 egg
140 g/5 oz plain flour, sifted
1 tsp baking powder
1 tsp bicarbonate of soda
140 g/5 oz rolled oats
30 g/1 oz bran
30 g/1 oz wheatgerm
85 g/3 oz mixed nuts, toasted
    and roughly chopped
175 g/6 oz plain chocolate chips
55 g/2 oz raisins and sultanas
175 g/6 oz plain chocolate,
    roughly chopped

method

1 Lightly grease 2 large baking sheets. In a large bowl, cream together the butter, sugar and egg. Add the flour, baking powder, bicarbonate of soda, oats, bran and wheatgerm and mix together until well combined. Stir in the nuts, chocolate chips and dried fruit.

2 Place 24 rounded tablespoonfuls of the biscuit mixture onto the prepared baking sheets. Transfer to a preheated oven, 180°C/350°F/Gas Mark 4, and bake for 12 minutes, or until the biscuits are golden brown.

3 Remove the biscuits from the oven, then transfer to a wire rack to cool completely. While they are cooling, put the chocolate pieces into a heatproof bowl over a saucepan of gently simmering water and heat until melted. Stir the chocolate, then cool slightly. Use a spoon to drizzle the chocolate in waves over the biscuits, or spoon it into a piping bag and pipe zigzag lines. Store in an airtight container in the refrigerator before serving.

white chocolate biscuits

ingredients

makes 24

125 g/4½ oz butter, softened,
   plus extra for greasing
125 g/4½ oz soft brown sugar
1 egg, beaten
200 g/7 oz self-raising flour
pinch of salt
125 g/4½ oz white chocolate,
   roughly chopped
50 g/1¾ oz Brazil nuts, chopped

method

1 Lightly grease 4 baking sheets. Beat the butter and sugar together in a large bowl until light and fluffy. Gradually add the beaten egg, beating well after each addition.

2 Sift the flour and salt into the creamed mixture and blend well. Stir in the white chocolate chunks and the chopped Brazil nuts.

3 Drop heaped teaspoons of the biscuit mixture onto the prepared baking sheets. Do not put more than 6 teaspoons onto each sheet as the biscuits will spread during cooking.

4 Bake in a preheated oven, 190°C/375°F/Gas Mark 5, for 10–12 minutes, or until just golden brown. Transfer the biscuits to wire racks and leave to cool completely before serving.

double chocolate chip cookies

ingredients

makes 24

200 g/7 oz butter, softened,
   plus extra for greasing
200 g/7 oz golden caster sugar
½ tsp vanilla extract
1 large egg
225 g/8 oz plain flour
pinch of salt
1 tsp bicarbonate of soda
115 g/4 oz white chocolate chips
115 g/4 oz plain chocolate chips

method

1 Lightly grease 2 large baking sheets. Place the butter, sugar and vanilla extract in a large bowl and beat together. Gradually beat in the egg until the cookie mixture is light and fluffy.

2 Sift the flour, salt and bicarbonate of soda over the cookie mixture and fold in the dry ingredients, then fold in the chocolate chips.

3 Place dessertspoonfuls of the cookie mixture onto the prepared baking sheets, allowing room for expansion during cooking. Bake in a preheated oven, 180°C/350°F/Gas Mark 4, for 10–12 minutes, or until crisp outside but still soft inside. Cool the cookies on the baking sheets for 2 minutes, then transfer to wire racks to cool completely.

chocolate chip oaties

ingredients

makes 20

115 g/4 oz butter, softened,
    plus extra for greasing
115 g/4 oz light brown sugar
1 egg
100 g/3½ oz rolled oats
1 tbsp milk
1 tsp vanilla extract
125 g/4½ oz plain flour
1 tbsp cocoa powder
½ tsp baking powder
175 g/6 oz plain chocolate,
    broken into pieces
175 g/6 oz milk chocolate,
    broken into pieces

method

1 Lightly grease 2 large baking sheets. Place the butter and sugar in a bowl and beat together until light and fluffy. Beat in the egg, then add the oats, milk and vanilla extract. Beat together until well blended. Sift the flour, cocoa powder and baking powder into the biscuit mixture and stir. Stir in the chocolate pieces.

2 Place dessertspoonfuls of the biscuit mixture onto the prepared baking sheets and flatten slightly with a fork. Bake in a preheated oven, 180°C/350°F/Gas Mark 4, for 15 minutes, or until slightly risen and firm to the touch. Let cool on the baking sheets for 2 minutes, then transfer to wire racks to cool completely.

apricot & chocolate chip cookies

ingredients

makes 12–14

85 g/3 oz butter, softened, plus
    extra for greasing
2 tbsp golden granulated sugar
55 g/2 oz light brown sugar
½ tsp vanilla extract
1 egg, beaten
175 g/6 oz self-raising flour
115 g/4 oz plain chocolate,
    roughly chopped
115 g/4 oz no-soak dried apricots,
    roughly chopped

method

1 Lightly grease 2 baking sheets. Place the butter, granulated sugar, brown sugar and vanilla extract in a bowl and beat together. Gradually beat in the egg until light and fluffy.

2 Sift the flour over the cookie mixture and fold in, then fold in the chocolate and apricots.

3 Place tablespoonfuls of the cookie mixture onto the prepared baking sheets, allowing space for the cookies to spread. Bake in a preheated oven, 180°C/350°F/Gas Mark 4, for 13–15 minutes, or until crisp outside but still soft inside. Cool on the baking sheets for 2 minutes, then transfer to wire racks to cool completely.

chocolate & apple oaties

ingredients

makes 24

115 g/4 oz apple sauce
2 tbsp apple juice
115 g/4 oz butter or margarine,
    plus extra for greasing
100 g/3½ oz brown sugar
1 tsp bicarbonate of soda
1 tsp almond essence
50 ml/2 fl oz boiling water
125 g/4½ oz rolled oats
280 g/10 oz plain flour, unsifted
pinch of salt
55 g/2 oz plain chocolate chips

method

1 Lightly grease 2 large baking sheets. Blend the apple sauce, apple juice, butter or margarine and sugar in a food processor until a fluffy consistency is reached.

2 In a separate bowl, mix together the bicarbonate of soda, almond essence and water, then add to the food processor and mix with the apple mixture. In another bowl, mix together the oats, flour and salt, then gradually stir into the apple mixture and beat well. Stir in the chocolate chips.

3 Place 24 rounded tablespoonfuls of mixture onto the prepared baking sheets, ensuring that they are well spaced. Transfer to a preheated oven, 200°C/400°F/Gas Mark 6, and bake for 15 minutes, or until the oaties are golden brown.

4 Remove the oaties from the oven, then transfer to a wire rack and cool completely before serving.

chocolate temptations

ingredients

makes 24

85 g/3 oz unsalted butter,
plus extra for greasing
365 g/12½ oz plain chocolate
1 tsp strong coffee
2 eggs
150 g/5 oz soft brown sugar
225 g/8 oz plain flour
¼ tsp baking powder
pinch of salt
2 tsp almond essence
50 g/1¾ oz Brazil nuts, chopped
50 g/1¾ oz hazelnuts, chopped
40 g/1½ oz white chocolate

method

1 Lightly grease 2 large baking sheets. Put 225 g/8 oz of the plain chocolate with the butter and coffee into a heatproof bowl over a saucepan of simmering water and heat until the chocolate is almost melted.

2 Meanwhile, beat the eggs in a bowl until fluffy. Whisk in the sugar gradually until thick. Remove the melted chocolate from the heat and stir until smooth, then stir it into the egg mixture until combined.

3 Sift the flour, baking powder and salt into a bowl and stir into the chocolate mixture. Chop 85 g/3 oz of plain chocolate into pieces and stir into the dough. Stir in the almond essence and nuts.

4 Put 24 rounded dessertspoonfuls of the dough onto the prepared baking sheets and bake in a preheated oven, 180°C/350°F/Gas Mark 4, for 16 minutes. Transfer the biscuits to a wire rack to cool. To decorate, melt the remaining chocolate (plain and white) in turn, then spoon into a piping bag and pipe lines across the biscuits.

lebkuchen

ingredients

makes 60

3 eggs
200 g/7 oz golden caster sugar
55 g/2 oz plain flour
2 tsp cocoa powder
1 tsp ground cinnamon
½ tsp ground cardamom
¼ tsp ground cloves
¼ tsp ground nutmeg
175 g/6 oz ground almonds
55 g/2 oz candied peel, finely
    chopped

to decorate

115 g/4 oz plain chocolate,
    melted and cooled
115 g/4 oz white chocolate,
    melted and cooled
sugar crystals

method

1 Line 3 large baking sheets with baking parchment. Place the eggs and sugar in a small heatproof bowl and set over a saucepan of gently simmering water. Whisk until thick and foamy. Remove the bowl from the pan and continue to whisk for 2 minutes.

2 Sift the flour, cocoa, cinnamon, cardamom, cloves and nutmeg over the egg mixture, add the ground almonds and chopped peel and stir. Drop heaped teaspoonfuls of the mixture onto the prepared baking sheets, spreading them gently into smooth mounds and allowing room for expansion during cooking.

3 Bake in a preheated oven, 160°C/325°F/Gas Mark 3, for 15–20 minutes, or until light brown and slightly soft to the touch. Cool on the baking sheets for 10 minutes, then transfer to wire racks to cool completely. Dip half the biscuits in the melted plain chocolate and half in the white chocolate. Sprinkle with sugar crystals, then allow to set before serving.

chequerboard biscuits

ingredients

makes 18

175 g/6 oz butter, softened,
    plus extra for greasing
85 g/3 oz icing sugar
1 teaspoon vanilla extract or
    grated rind of ½ orange
250 g/9 oz plain flour
25 g/1 oz plain chocolate
a little beaten egg white

method

1 Beat the butter and icing sugar in a mixing bowl until light and fluffy. Beat in the vanilla extract or grated orange rind. Gradually beat in the flour to form a soft dough. Use your fingers to incorporate the last of the flour and bring the dough together.

2 Melt the chocolate. Divide the dough in half and beat the melted chocolate into one half. Keeping each half of the dough separate, cover and chill for 30 minutes.

3 Lightly grease a large baking sheet. Roll out each piece of dough to a rectangle measuring 7.5 x 20 cm/3 x 8 inches and 3-cm/1¼-inches thick. Brush one piece of dough with a little egg white and place the other on top. Cut the block of dough in half lengthways and turn over one half. Brush the side of one strip with egg white and butt the other up to it, so that it resembles a chequerboard.

4 Cut the block into thin slices and place each slice flat on the prepared baking sheet, allowing enough room for the slices to spread out a little during cooking.

5 Bake in a preheated oven, 180°C/350°F/Gas Mark 4, for 10 minutes, or until just firm to the touch. Cool the biscuits on the baking sheets for a few minutes, before transferring with a spatula, to a wire rack to cool completely.

caramel chocolate shortbread

ingredients

makes 12

115 g/4 oz butter, plus extra
    for greasing
175 g/6 oz plain flour
55 g/2 oz golden caster sugar

filling and topping

175 g/6 oz butter
115 g/4 oz golden caster sugar
3 tbsp golden syrup
400 g/14 oz canned condensed
    milk
200 g/7 oz plain chocolate,
    broken into pieces

method

1 Grease and base-line a 23-cm/9-inch shallow square cake tin.

2 Place the butter, flour and sugar in a food processor and process until it begins to bind together. Press the mixture into the prepared tin and smooth the top. Bake in a preheated oven, 180°C/350°F/Gas Mark 4, for 20–25 minutes, or until golden.

3 Meanwhile, make the filling. Place the butter, sugar, syrup and condensed milk in a saucepan and heat gently until the sugar has melted. Bring to the boil and simmer for 6–8 minutes, stirring constantly, until the mixture becomes very thick. Pour over the shortbread base and chill in the refrigerator until firm to the touch.

4 To make the topping, melt the chocolate and leave to cool, then spread over the caramel. Chill in the refrigerator until set. Cut the shortbread into 12 pieces with a sharp knife and serve.

cappuccino squares

ingredients

makes 15

225 g/8 oz self-raising flour
1 tsp baking powder
1 tsp cocoa powder, plus extra
   for dusting
225 g/8 oz butter, softened,
   plus extra for greasing
225 g/8 oz golden caster sugar
4 eggs, beaten
3 tbsp instant coffee powder,
   dissolved in 2 tbsp hot water

white chocolate frosting

115 g/4 oz white chocolate,
   broken into pieces
55 g/2 oz butter, softened
3 tbsp milk
175 g/6 oz icing sugar

method

1 Lightly grease and base-line a shallow 28 x 18-cm/
   11 x 7-inch cake tin.

2 Sift the flour, baking powder and cocoa into a bowl
   and add the butter, caster sugar, eggs and coffee. Beat
   well, by hand or using an electric whisk, until smooth,
   then spoon the mixture into the prepared tin and
   smooth the top.

3 Bake in a preheated oven, 180°C/350°F/Gas Mark 4,
   for 35–40 minutes, or until risen and firm to the touch,
   then turn out onto a wire rack, and cool completely.

4 To make the frosting, place the chocolate, butter and
   milk in a bowl set over a saucepan of simmering water
   and stir until the chocolate has melted. Remove the
   bowl from the pan and sift in the icing sugar. Beat until
   smooth, then spread over the cake. Dust the top of the
   cake with sifted cocoa, then cut into squares.

chocolate fudge brownies

ingredients

makes 16

200 g/7 oz low-fat soft cheese
½ tsp vanilla extract
250 g/9 oz caster sugar
2 eggs
100 g/3½ oz butter, plus extra
  for greasing
3 tbsp cocoa powder
100 g/3½ oz self-raising flour,
  sifted
50 g/1¾ oz chopped pecan nuts

fudge frosting

50 g/2 oz butter
1 tbsp milk
100 g/3½ oz icing sugar
2 tbsp cocoa powder
pecan nuts, to decorate

method

1 Lightly grease a 20-cm/8-inch square shallow cake tin.

2 Beat together the cheese, vanilla extract and 5 teaspoons of caster sugar, then set aside.

3 Beat the eggs and remaining caster sugar together until light and fluffy. Place the butter and cocoa powder in a small saucepan and heat gently, stirring until the butter melts and the mixture combines, then stir it into the egg mixture. Fold in the flour and nuts.

4 Pour half of the brownie mixture into the prepared tin and smooth the top. Carefully spread the soft cheese over it, then cover it with the remaining brownie mixture. Bake in a preheated oven, 180°C/350°F/Gas Mark 4, for 40–45 minutes. Leave to cool in the tin.

5 To make the frosting, melt the butter in the milk. Stir in the sugar and cocoa. Using a spatula, spread the frosting over the brownies and decorate with pecan nuts. Let the frosting set, then cut into squares to serve.

mocha brownies

ingredients

makes 16

115 g/4 oz plain chocolate,
   broken into pieces
55 g/2 oz butter, plus extra
   for greasing
175 g/6 oz brown sugar
2 eggs
1 tbsp instant coffee powder,
   dissolved in 1 tbsp hot water,
   cooled
85 g/3 oz plain flour
½ tsp baking powder
55 g/2 oz roughly chopped
   pecan nuts

method

1 Lightly grease and base-line a 20-cm/8-inch square
   cake tin.

2 Place the chocolate and butter in a heavy-based
   saucepan over low heat until melted. Stir and set
   aside to cool.

3 Place the sugar and eggs in a large bowl and cream
   together until light and fluffy. Fold in the chocolate
   mixture and cooled coffee and mix thoroughly. Sift in
   the flour and baking powder and lightly fold into the
   mixture, then carefully fold in the pecan nuts.

4 Pour the mixture into the prepared tin and bake in a
   preheated oven, 180°C/350°F/Gas Mark 4, for 25–30
   minutes, or until firm and a skewer inserted into the
   centre comes out clean.

5 Cool in the tin for a few minutes, then run a knife
   round the edge of the cake to loosen it. Turn the cake
   out onto a wire rack, peel off the lining paper, and cool
   completely. When cold, cut into squares and serve.

refrigerator cake

ingredients

makes 12

55 g/2 oz raisins

2 tbsp brandy

115 g/4 oz plain chocolate,
broken into pieces

115 g/4 oz milk chocolate,
broken into pieces

55 g/2 oz butter, plus extra
for greasing

2 tbsp golden syrup

175 g/6 oz digestive biscuits,
roughly broken

55 g/2 oz flaked almonds,
lightly toasted

25 g/1 oz glacé cherries, chopped

topping

100 g/3½ oz plain chocolate,
broken into pieces

20 g/¾ oz butter

method

1 Lightly grease and base-line a 18-cm/7-inch shallow
square tin.

2 Place the raisins and brandy in a bowl and soak for
30 minutes. Put the chocolate, butter and syrup in
a saucepan and heat gently, stirring, until melted.

3 Stir in the digestive biscuits, almonds, cherries, raisins
and brandy. Turn the mixture into the prepared tin
and leave to cool. Cover and chill in the refrigerator for
1 hour.

4 To make the topping, place the chocolate and butter
in a small heatproof bowl and melt over a saucepan
of gently simmering water. Stir and pour the chocolate
mixture over the biscuit base. Chill in the refrigerator
for 8 hours, or overnight. Cut into bars or squares
to serve.

chocolates & petits fours

chocolate almond petits fours

ingredients

serves 16

40 g/1½ oz ground almonds
85 g/3 oz granulated sugar
5 tsp cocoa powder
1 egg white
8 blanched almonds, halved
55 g/2 oz plain chocolate, broken
    in pieces

method

1 Line a baking tray with baking parchment paper.

2 Put the ground almonds, sugar and cocoa powder in a bowl and mix together well. Add the egg white and mix to form a firm mixture.

3 Fill a piping bag, fitted with a small plain nozzle, with the mixture and pipe 5-cm/2-inch lengths, spaced well apart, onto the prepared baking tray. Place an almond half on top of each.

4 Bake in a preheated oven, 190°C/375°F/Gas Mark 5, for about 5 minutes, or until firm to the touch. Transfer to a wire rack and leave to cool completely.

5 When the petits fours are cold, melt the chocolate in a heatproof bowl set over a saucepan of gently simmering water. Dip each end of the petits fours into the melted chocolate, then leave on the wire rack to set.

chocolate creams

ingredients

makes 30

200 g/7 oz plain chocolate, broken into pieces
2 tbsp single cream
225 g/8 oz icing sugar
cocoa powder, for dusting

method

1 Line a baking tray with baking parchment paper.

2 Melt 55 g/2 oz of the chocolate in a large heatproof bowl set over a saucepan of gently simmering water. Stir in the cream and remove the bowl from the heat.

3 Sift the icing sugar into the melted chocolate then, using a fork, mix together well. Knead to form a firm, smooth, pliable mixture.

4 Lightly dust a work surface with cocoa powder, turn out the mixture, and roll out to a 5-mm/¼-inch thickness, then cut into rounds, using a 2.5-cm/1-inch plain round cutter.

5 Transfer the rounds to the prepared baking tray and leave to stand for about 12 hours, or overnight, until dry and set.

6 Melt the remaining chocolate in a heatproof bowl set over a saucepan of gently simmering water. Using 2 forks, carefully dip each chocolate cream into the melted chocolate. Lift it out quickly, letting any excess chocolate drain against the side of the bowl, and place on the prepared baking tray. Leave to set.

ginger chocolate fudge

ingredients

makes 50

6 pieces stem ginger, plus extra
　for decorating (optional)
300 ml/10 fl oz milk
150 g/5½ oz plain chocolate,
　broken into pieces
115 g/4 oz butter, plus extra
　for greasing
450 g/1 lb granulated sugar

method

1 Lightly grease an 18-cm/7-inch square, shallow tin
　or a 20 x 15-cm/8 x 6-inch rectangular, shallow tin.

2 Dry the syrup off the pieces of stem ginger on kitchen
　paper, then chop the ginger finely.

3 Pour the milk into a large, heavy-based saucepan
　and add the chocolate, butter and sugar. Heat gently,
　stirring all the time, until the chocolate and butter
　have melted and the sugar has completely dissolved.

4 Bring to the boil and boil for about 10–15 minutes,
　stirring occasionally, until a little of the mixture, when
　dropped into a small bowl of cold water, forms a soft
　ball when rolled between the fingers.

5 Remove the saucepan from the heat and stir in the
　chopped ginger. Leave to cool for 5 minutes, then beat
　the mixture vigorously with a wooden spoon, until
　thick, creamy and grainy.

6 Immediately pour the mixture into the prepared tin,
　leave to cool, then mark into small squares. Leave the
　fudge until cold and set, then cut up into squares with
　a sharp knife. Decorate with ginger, if wished.

easy chocolate fudge

ingredients

makes 25

500 g/1 lb 2 oz plain chocolate
75 g/2¾ oz unsalted butter, cut
    into even-size pieces, plus
    extra for greasing
400 g/14 oz canned sweetened
    condensed milk
½ tsp vanilla extract

method

1 Lightly grease a 20-cm/8-inch square cake tin with butter.

2 Break the chocolate into small pieces and place in a large, heavy-based saucepan with the butter and condensed milk.

3 Heat gently, stirring constantly, until the chocolate and butter melt and the mixture is smooth. Do not allow to boil. Remove from the heat. Beat in the vanilla extract, then beat the mixture for a few minutes until thickened. Pour the mixture into the prepared tin and level the top.

4 Chill the mixture in the refrigerator for 1 hour, or until firm to the touch. Tip the fudge out onto a chopping board and cut into squares to serve.

pecan mocha fudge

ingredients

makes 80

300 ml/10 fl oz milk

1 kg/2 lb 4 oz golden granulated
sugar

250 g/9 oz butter, plus extra
for greasing

2 tbsp instant coffee granules

2 tbsp cocoa powder

2 tbsp golden syrup

400 g/14 oz canned condensed
milk

115 g/4 oz shelled pecan nuts,
chopped

method

1 Lightly grease a 30 x 23-cm/12 x 9-inch Swiss roll tin.

2 Place the milk, sugar and butter in a large saucepan.
Stir over gentle heat until the sugar has dissolved.
Stir in the coffee granules, cocoa, syrup and
condensed milk.

3 Bring to the boil and boil steadily, whisking constantly,
for 10 minutes, or until a temperature of 116°C/241°F
has been reached on a sugar thermometer, or a small
amount of the mixture forms a soft ball when dropped
into cold water.

4 Cool for 5 minutes, then beat vigorously with a
wooden spoon until the mixture starts to thicken.
Stir in the nuts. Continue beating until the mixture
takes on a fudge-like consistency. Quickly pour into
the prepared tin and stand in a cool place to set.
Cut the fudge into squares to serve.

white chocolate truffles

ingredients

makes 12

25 g/1 oz unsalted butter
75 ml/2½ fl oz double cream
225 g/8 oz good-quality Swiss
    white chocolate
1 tbsp orange-flavoured liqueur
    (optional)

to finish
100 g/3½ oz white chocolate

method

1 Line a Swiss roll tin with a sheet of baking parchment.

2 Place the butter and cream in a small saucepan and bring slowly to the boil, stirring constantly. Boil the mixture for 1 minute, then remove the pan from the heat.

3 Break the chocolate into pieces and add to the cream. Stir until melted, then beat in the orange-flavoured liqueur, if using. Pour into the prepared tin and chill for about 2 hours, or until firm to the touch.

4 Break off pieces of the truffle mixture and roll them into balls. Chill for a further 30 minutes before finishing the truffles.

5 To finish, melt the white chocolate in a bowl set over a saucepan of gently simmering water. Dip the balls in the chocolate, allowing the excess to drip back into the bowl. Place in the prepared tin, swirl the chocolate with the tines of a fork, and leave to harden.

variation

Use 100 g/3½ oz plain or milk chocolate instead of the white chocolate to finish the truffles.

irish cream truffles

ingredients

makes 24

150 ml/5 fl oz double cream
225 g/8 oz plain chocolate,
    broken into pieces
25 g/1 oz butter
3 tbsp Irish cream liqueur

to finish

115 g/4 oz white chocolate,
    broken into pieces
115 g/4 oz plain chocolate,
    broken into pieces

method

1 Heat the cream in a saucepan over low heat but do not allow it to boil. Remove from the heat and stir in the chocolate and butter. Stand for 2 minutes, then stir until smooth. Stir in the liqueur. Pour the mixture into a bowl and cool. Cover with clingfilm and chill in the refrigerator for 8 hours, overnight, or until firm to the touch.

2 Line a baking sheet with baking parchment. Take teaspoonfuls of the chilled chocolate mixture and roll into small balls. Place the balls on the prepared baking sheet and chill in the refrigerator for 2–4 hours, or until firm to the touch. Melt the white chocolate pieces and cool slightly.

3 Coat half the truffles by spearing on thin skewers or cocktail sticks and dipping into the white chocolate. Transfer onto the prepared baking sheet to set. Melt the plain chocolate and cool slightly, then use to coat the remaining truffles in the same way. Store the truffles in the refrigerator in an airtight container, separated by layers of waxed paper, for up to 1 week.

rum truffles

ingredients

makes 12

125 g/4½ oz plain chocolate
small piece of butter
2 tbsp rum
50 g/1¾ oz shredded coconut
100 g/3½ oz cake crumbs
70 g/2½ oz icing sugar
2 tbsp cocoa powder

method

1 Line a baking sheet with baking parchment. Break the chocolate into pieces and place in a bowl with the butter. Set the bowl over a saucepan of gently simmering water and stir until melted and combined.

2 Remove from the heat and beat in the rum. Stir in the shredded coconut, cake crumbs and two-thirds of the icing sugar. Beat until combined. Add a little extra rum if the mixture is stiff.

3 Roll the mixture into small balls and place them onto the prepared baking sheet. Chill in the refrigerator until firm to the touch.

4 Sieve the remaining icing sugar onto a large plate. Sieve the cocoa powder onto another plate. Roll half of the truffles in the icing sugar until thoroughly coated and roll the remaining rum truffles in the cocoa.

5 Place the truffles in paper petit four cases or arrange on a plate and chill in the refrigerator.

chocolate orange collettes

ingredients

makes 20

280 g/10 oz plain chocolate,
    broken into pieces
½ tsp corn oil
150 ml/5 fl oz double cream
finely grated rind of ½ orange
1 tbsp Cointreau

to decorate

chopped nuts
fine strips of orange rind

method

1 Melt 150 g/5½ oz of the chocolate with the oil and stir until mixed. Spread evenly over the inside of 20 double-layer petit four cases, taking care to keep a good thickness round the edge. Chill for one hour, or until set, then apply a second coat of chocolate, remelting if necessary. Chill for 1 hour, or until set.

2 Place the cream and grated orange rind in a saucepan and heat until almost boiling. Remove from the heat, add the remaining chocolate pieces and stir until smooth. Return to the heat and stir until the mixture starts to bubble. Remove from the heat and stir in the Cointreau, then cool. Peel the paper cases off the chocolate cups.

3 Beat the chocolate cream until thick, then spoon into a large piping bag fitted with a fluted nozzle. Pipe the chocolate cream into the chocolate cases. Decorate some of the chocolate collettes with chopped nuts and some with a few strips of orange rind. Cover and keep in the refrigerator. Use within 2–3 days.

chocolate liqueurs

ingredients

makes 20

100 g/3½ oz plain chocolate
5 glacé cherries, halved
10 hazelnuts or macadamia nuts
150 ml/5 fl oz double cream
2 tbsp icing sugar
4 tbsp liqueur

to finish

50 g/1¾ oz plain chocolate, melted
a little white chocolate, melted, or
    white chocolate curls, or extra
    nuts and cherries

method

1 Line a baking sheet with a sheet of baking parchment. Break the plain chocolate into pieces, place in a bowl and set over a saucepan of hot water. Stir until melted. Spoon the chocolate into 20 double-layer paper petit four cases, spreading up the sides with a small spoon or brush. Place upside down on the baking sheet and leave to set.

2 Carefully peel away the paper cases. Place a cherry or nut in the bottom of each cup.

3 To make the filling, place the double cream in a mixing bowl and sift the icing sugar on top. Whisk the cream until it is just holding its shape, then whisk in the liqueur to flavour it.

4 Place the cream in a piping bag fitted with a 1-cm/½-inch plain nozzle and pipe a little into each chocolate case. Chill for 20 minutes.

5 To finish, spoon the plain chocolate over the cream to cover it and pipe the melted white chocolate on top, swirling it into the plain chocolate with a cocktail stick. Set aside to harden. Alternatively, cover the cream with the melted plain chocolate and decorate with white chocolate curls before setting. If you prefer, place a small piece of nut or cherry on top of the cream, then cover with plain chocolate.

chocolate mascarpone cups

ingredients

makes 20

100 g/3½ oz plain chocolate

filling

100 g/3½ oz milk or plain
    chocolate
200 g/7 oz mascarpone cheese
¼ tsp vanilla extract
cocoa powder, for dusting

method

1 Line a baking sheet with a sheet of baking parchment.
Break the plain chocolate into pieces, place in a bowl
and set over a saucepan of hot water. Stir until melted.
Spoon the chocolate into 20 double-layer paper petit
four cases, spreading up the sides with a small spoon
or brush. Place the chocolate cups upside down on the
baking sheet and leave to set. When set, carefully peel
away the paper cases.

2 To make the filling, melt the chocolate. Place the
mascarpone cheese in a bowl and beat in the vanilla
extract and melted chocolate until well combined.
Chill the mixture in the refrigerator, beating occasionally,
until firm enough to pipe.

3 Place the mascarpone filling in a piping bag fitted
with a star nozzle and pipe the mixture into the cups.
Finish with a dusting of cocoa.

mini chocolate cones

ingredients

makes 10

75 g/2¾ oz plain chocolate
100 ml/3½ fl oz double cream
1 tbsp icing sugar
1 tbsp crème de menthe
chocolate-covered coffee beans,
    to decorate (optional)

method

1 Cut 10 x 7.5-cm/3-inch circles of baking parchment. Shape each circle into a cone shape and secure with a piece of sticky tape.

2 Break the chocolate into pieces, place in a heatproof bowl and set over a pan of hot water. Stir until the chocolate has melted. Using a small pastry brush or clean artist's brush, brush the inside of each cone with the melted chocolate.

3 Brush a second layer of chocolate on the inside of the cones and chill in the refrigerator for 2 hours, or until set. Carefully peel away the paper.

4 Place the cream, icing sugar and crème de menthe in a large bowl and whip until just holding its shape. Place in a piping bag fitted with a star nozzle and pipe the mixture into the chocolate cones. Decorate the cones with chocolate-covered coffee beans, if using, and chill in the refrigerator for 1–2 hours.

brazil nut brittle

ingredients

makes 20

oil, for brushing
350 g/12 oz plain chocolate,
    broken into pieces
85 g/3 oz shelled Brazil nuts,
    chopped
175 g/6 oz white chocolate,
    coarsely chopped
175 g/6 oz fudge, roughly chopped

method

1 Brush the bottom of a 20-cm/8-inch square cake tin with oil and line with baking parchment. Melt half the plain chocolate and spread in the prepared tin.

2 Sprinkle with the chopped Brazil nuts, white chocolate and fudge. Melt the remaining plain chocolate pieces and pour over the top.

3 Leave the brittle to set, then break up into jagged pieces using the tip of a strong knife.

nutty chocolate clusters

ingredients

makes 30

175 g/6 oz white chocolate
100 g/3½ oz digestive biscuits
100 g/3½ oz chopped macadamia
   nuts or brazil nuts
25 g/1 oz stem ginger, chopped
   (optional)
175 g/6 oz plain chocolate

method

1 Line a baking sheet with a sheet of baking parchment. Break the white chocolate into small pieces and melt in a mixing bowl set over a saucepan of gently simmering water.

2 Break the digestive biscuits into small pieces. Stir the biscuits into the melted chocolate with the chopped nuts and stem ginger, if using.

3 Place heaped teaspoons of the chocolate cluster mixture onto the prepared baking sheet. Chill in the refrigerator until set, then carefully remove from the baking parchment.

4 Melt the plain chocolate and cool slightly. Dip the clusters into the chocolate, letting the excess drip back into the bowl. Return to the baking sheet and chill until set.

apricot & almond clusters

ingredients

makes 24–28

115 g/4 oz plain chocolate,
   broken into pieces
2 tbsp honey
115 g/4 oz no-soak dried apricots,
   chopped
55 g/2 oz blanched almonds,
   chopped

method

1 Place the chocolate and honey in a bowl and set
   over a saucepan of gently simmering water until the
   chocolate has melted. Stir in the apricots and almonds.

2 Drop teaspoonfuls of the mixture into petit four cases.
   Leave to set for 2–4 hours, or until firm to the touch.

chocolate cherries

ingredients

makes 24

12 glacé cherries
2 tbsp rum or brandy
250 g/9 oz marzipan
125 g/5½ oz plain chocolate
extra milk, plain or white
    chocolate, to decorate

method

1 Cut the glacé cherries in half and place in a small bowl. Add the rum or brandy and stir to coat. Let the cherries soak for at least 1 hour, stirring occasionally.

2 Line a baking sheet with a sheet of baking parchment. Divide the marzipan into 24 pieces and roll each piece into a ball. Press half a cherry into the top of each marzipan ball.

3 Break the chocolate into pieces, place in a bowl, and set over a saucepan of hot water. Stir until melted. Dip each marzipan ball into the melted chocolate using a toothpick, allowing the excess to drip back into the bowl. Place the coated cherries on the baking parchment and chill in the refrigerator until set.

4 Melt a little extra chocolate and drizzle it over the top of the coated cherries. Set aside until set.

ladies' kisses

ingredients

makes 20

140 g/5 oz unsalted butter
115 g/4 oz caster sugar
1 egg yolk
115 g/4 oz ground almonds
175 g/6 oz plain flour
55 g/2 oz plain chocolate,
  broken into pieces
2 tbsp icing sugar
2 tbsp cocoa powder

method

1 Beat the butter and sugar together in a bowl until pale and fluffy. Beat in the egg yolk, then beat in the almonds and flour. Continue beating until well mixed. Shape the dough into a ball, wrap in clingfilm and chill in the refrigerator for 1½–2 hours.

2 Line 3 baking sheets with baking parchment. Unwrap the dough, break off walnut-size pieces, and roll them into balls between the palms of your hands. Place the dough balls on the prepared sheets, allowing room for expansion during cooking. Bake in a preheated oven, 160°C/325°F/Gas Mark 3, for 20–25 minutes, or until golden brown. Carefully transfer the biscuits, still on the baking parchment, to wire racks to cool completely.

3 Place the plain chocolate in a small heatproof bowl and set over a saucepan of barely simmering water, stirring constantly, until melted. Remove from the heat.

4 Remove the biscuits from the baking parchment, and spread the melted chocolate over the bases. Sandwich them together in pairs and return to the wire racks to cool. Dust with icing sugar and cocoa powder and serve.

variation

Use 115 g/4 oz of ground hazelnuts instead of the ground almonds.

mini florentines

ingredients

makes 40

85 g/3 oz butter, plus extra
   for greasing
75 g/2¾ oz caster sugar
2 tbsp sultanas or raisins
2 tbsp chopped glacé cherries
2 tbsp chopped crystallized ginger
25 g/1 oz sunflower seeds
100 g/3½ oz flaked almonds
2 tbsp double cream
175 g/6 oz plain chocolate

method

1 Lightly grease and flour 2 baking sheets or line them
   with baking parchment.

2 Gently heat the butter in a small saucepan until melted.
   Add the sugar, stir until dissolved, then bring the
   mixture to the boil. Remove from the heat and stir in
   the sultanas, cherries, ginger, sunflower seeds and
   almonds. Mix well, then beat in the cream.

3 Place small teaspoons of the fruit and nut mixture onto
   the prepared baking sheets, allowing plenty of space
   for the mixture to spread. Bake in a preheated oven,
   180°C/350°F/Gas Mark 4, for 10–12 minutes, or until
   light golden in colour. Remove from the oven and,
   while still hot, use a circular biscuit cutter to pull in the
   edges to form perfect circles. Let the florentines cool
   and go crisp before removing from the baking sheet.

4 Break the chocolate into pieces, place in a bowl over
   a saucepan of hot water and stir until melted. Spread
   most of the chocolate onto a sheet of baking parchment.
   When the chocolate is nearly set, place the florentines
   flat-side down on the chocolate and leave to harden.

5 Cut around the florentines and remove from the
   baking parchment. Spread a little more chocolate
   on the coated side of the florentines and use a fork to
   mark waves in the chocolate. Leave to set and keep cool.

chocolate biscotti

ingredients

makes 16

butter, for greasing
1 egg
100 g/3½ oz caster sugar
1 tsp vanilla extract
125 g/5½ oz plain flour
½ tsp baking powder
1 tsp ground cinnamon
50 g/1¾ oz plain chocolate,
   roughly chopped
50 g/1¾ oz toasted flaked almonds
50 g/1¾ oz pine nuts

method

1 Lightly grease a large baking sheet. Whisk the egg, sugar and vanilla extract in a mixing bowl with an electric mixer until thick – ribbons of mixture should trail from the whisk as you lift it.

2 Sift the flour, baking powder and cinnamon into a separate bowl, then sift into the egg mixture and fold in gently. Stir in the chopped plain chocolate, toasted flaked almonds and pine nuts.

3 Turn the mixture out onto a lightly floured work surface and shape into a flat log, 23 cm/9 inches long and 1.5 cm/¾ inch wide. Transfer to the prepared baking sheet.

4 Bake in a preheated oven, 180°C/350°F/Gas Mark 4, for 20–25 minutes, or until golden. Remove the log from the oven and cool for 5 minutes, or until firm to the touch.

5 Transfer the log to a chopping board. Using a serrated bread knife, cut the log on the diagonal into slices about 1 cm/½ inch thick and arrange them on the prepared baking sheet. Cook for 10–15 minutes, turning halfway through the cooking time.

6 Cool for 5 minutes on the baking sheet, then transfer to a wire rack to cool completely.

index